D0897838

STUDIES IN ECONOMIC AND SOCIAL HISTORY

This series, specially commissioned by the Economic History Society, provides a guide to the current interpretations of the key themes of economic and social history in which advances have recently been made or in which there has been significant debate.

Originally entitled 'Studies in Economic History', in 1974 the series had its scope extended to include topics in social history, and the new series title, 'Studies in Economic and Social History', signalises this development.

The series gives readers access to the best work done, helps them to draw their own conclusions in major fields of study, and by means of the critical bibliography in each book guides them in the selection of further reading. The aim is to provide a springboard to further work rather than a set of pre-packaged conclusions or short-cuts.

ECONOMIC HISTORY SOCIETY

The Economic History Society, which numbers over 3000 members, publishes the *Economic History Review* four times a year (free to members) and holds an annual conference. Enquiries about membership should be addressed to the Assistant Secretary, Economic History Society, Peterhouse, Cambridge. Full-time students may join the Society at special rates.

STUDIES IN ECONOMIC AND SOCIAL HISTORY

Edited for the Economic History Society by M. W. Flinn

PUBLISHED

OTHER TITLES ARE IN PREPARATION

Internal Trade in England
1500–1700

Prepared for
The Economic History Society by

J. A. CHARTRES

Lecturer in Economic History,
University of Leeds

P 21

First published 1977 by
THE MACMILLAN PRESS LTD
London and Basingstoke
Associated companies in New York Dublin
Melbourne Johannesburg and Madras

ISBN 0 333 18358 4

Phototypeset by
WESTERN PRINTING SERVICES LTD
Bristol

Printed in Great Britain by
REDWOOD BURN LIMITED
Trowbridge & Esher

Contents

Acknowledgements

I wish to thank friends and colleagues John Bowers, John Broad, Christopher Challis, Patricia Hudson, Gerard Turnbull and Donald Woodward for their comments on an earlier draft. Two students, Margaret Robb and Stephen Verde, kindly acted as 'guinea pigs'. Professor T. S. Willan generously advised me of the content of his then forthcoming book, and the Editor must be thanked for his patience and many common-sense suggestions.

Note on References

References in the text within square brackets relate to the numbered items in the Select Bibliography, followed, where necessary, by the page numbers in italics: for example [3, *782*]. Other references in the text, numbered consecutively throughout the book, relate to annotations of the text or to sources not given in the Select Bibliography, and are itemised in the Notes and References section.

Editor's Preface

RECOGNISING the need for guidance through the burgeoning and confusing literature that has grown around many of the major topics in economic and social history, the Economic History Society hopes in this series of short books to offer some help to students and teachers. The books are intended to serve as guides to current interpretations in major fields of economic and social history in which important advances have recently been made, or in which there has recently been some significant debate. Each book aims to survey recent work, to indicate the full scope of the particular problem as it has been opened up by recent scholarship, and to draw such conclusions as seem warranted, given the present state of knowledge and understanding. The authors will often be at pains to point out where, in their view, because of a lack of information or inadequate research, they believe it is premature to attempt to draw firm conclusions. While authors will not hesitate to review recent and older work critically, the books are not intended to serve as vehicles for their own specialist views: the aim is to provide a balanced summary rather than an exposition of the author's own viewpoint. Each book will include a descriptive bibliography. Above all, the aim is to help the reader to draw his own conclusions, and to guide him in the selection of further reading as a means to this end, rather than to present him with a set of pre-packaged conclusions.

M. W. FLINN
Editor

1 The Problem of Internal Trade

FEW political economists before Daniel Defoe, writing at the close of our period, acknowledged the macroeconomic significance of internal trade in England. Contemporary economic literature tended to be concerned with matters of international trade or with the currency issues related to it. Politicians and commentators were often prepared to indict the middleman or the level of domestic consumption for the felony of trade depression, but few seem to have accepted that the domestic trades performed valuable and even vital economic functions. Little wonder, therefore, that Defoe felt the need to write of the home trades in somewhat evangelical fashion [6].

Until relatively recently, economic historians have tended to fall into the same trap. Like good mercantilists, they have looked primarily to overseas trades and the export market as the sources of the moderate economic growth which characterised the seventeenth century, and which forms the essential analytical background to studies of the causation of the Industrial Revolution. Classically, the colonial/tropical trade-based 'Commercial Revolution' of the later seventeenth century has been seen as the major precursor of home developments, generating incomes from trade and shifting the demand schedule [13]. To these may be added the 'spin-off' effects in shipbuilding or financial institutions which may have been more important than simple 'gains-from-trade' [10, *218 f.*]. To the present, the home market has been credited with a more or less passive role in this process of growth.

Such views stem principally from a basic problem in studying trade in the past, the danger of attributing to the survival of data an undue weight. Medieval and early modern scholarship, as Postan warned, is particularly susceptible to this logical error, which accounts in part for the curious neglect of inland trade in the economic history of sixteenth- and seventeenth-century England. Because overseas trade has generated a copious, if problematical, volume of statistical materials, historians may have been led to look more closely at the external account than the over-all balance of the economy would warrant. In consequence, it is not easy to guide students through the literature on inland trade in this period, since the body of scholarly work is itself rather thin. Of necessity, therefore, this study will have to follow references which point to particular rather than general conclusions. As well as being a guide to current interpretations, it must be regarded as a plea for more work on the subject.

In the absence even of crude measures of Gross National Product for the bulk of this period, it is difficult to establish the magnitude of internal trade relative to that of the roughly-quantifiable external exchange. The first such analysis was based by Deane and Cole on the work of that enthusiastic arithmetician, Gregory King, and applied to the year 1688. The home market, exclusive of agricultural commodities, but including distribution and transport, may have accounted for £10·5m. of a total national income of c. £50m. or 21 per cent. In addition, some 40 per cent or more of G.N.P. was attributable to agriculture, which, despite its improving export performance in the late seventeenth century, remained largely the subject of transactions in the home market [11]. Against this, exports can have held no more than 10 per cent of G.N.P. in King's survey of 1688, and exports and imports together no more than 15 per cent exclusive of re-exports [12]. In terms of direct generation of incomes, the home market was dominant in 1688.

Little can be added to these rough-and-ready workings from a source of unknown reliability in the retrospective analysis to 1500. External trades may have been as much as five times greater in 1700 than in 1500 [10] but even in the dominant export commodity, woollen manufactures, it seems unlikely that overseas trade absorbed more than half of total output. A contemporary estimate suggested that the home market for cloths was 61 per cent in 1618–19.[1] Allowing for changes in incomes and overseas demand, it is still hard to attribute more than half the output of woollens to export trades c.1500, even if this picture might be different in value, not volume, terms. Despite the lack of certain figures, it seems clear that even in this predominant component of domestic exports, the home market was at least as important a destination.

From this it follows that in terms of employment the home market was of vital importance, and that internal trade handled perhaps a quarter or a third of G.N.P. in the sixteenth and seventeenth centuries. The bulk of incomes from employment were dependent upon home trades and services, and for the great majority of their producers, the state of internal trade was of immediate concern. Through internal trade was expressed the impact of the basic source of economic fluctuations, that of the harvest [74–7] and of the consumption released, seasonally, from the agricultural sector. The vast bulk of manufactures, much of the product of the mineral and extractive industries, of the fishing and of the importing industries, was also traded domestically. No assessment of the English economy in this period can be complete without an analysis of the state and development of internal trade. By many measures, it was of greater significance than the foreign trades which have been discussed so much more extensively by economic historians, for this latter view must be regarded as an error of emphasis, albeit an understandable one.

Naturally, one must not attribute to this relative dominance of internal over foreign trade the same proportionate weight in generating growth in the economy. Most analysts of the slow growth of the economy from the mid-sixteenth century have attributed the principal dynamic role to foreign trade, especially to the re-export trade in colonial and tropical goods, and in the indirect or 'spin-off' effects on the structure of home industries and business institutions. But the contribution of exports and re-exports to G.N.P. in this period was little greater than the value of imports, and it is tempting, with J. F. Wright, to stress the role of widened consumer choice in this growth.[2] Such a Malthusian growth model would further stress imports, and the function of the internal trading network, which distributed and marketed them. While external trade was very important to the economy, the direct influences for slow structural change and for more efficient employment of factors were those of internal commerce.

In sum, the study of internal trades is of considerable significance in the period 1500–1700. The greater part of G.N.P. seems to have been generated internally, and the great bulk of domestic products was destined for the home market. Through transport and distribution, internal trade contributed a very substantial proportion of domestic value added, and this proportion may have grown between 1500 and 1700. Additionally, the function of internal trade as a vehicle of economic growth in this period requires re-assessment. All of which suggests that the familiar logical error among historians, that of imputing a trend to the mere existence of data, may have been displayed in surveying the

English economy in this period. Despite the paucity of consistent data, and the consequent lack of general scholarly interest, it is essential to analyse the home trades if we are to understand English economic development from 1500 to 1700.

2 The Profile of the Internal Trades

THE contrast between the foreign and the domestic trades is as sharp in terms of surviving data as in the amount of academic interest the two have generated. Internal trade was largely untaxed in the period 1500–1700, or bore only moderate dues, such as the brokage tolls of Southampton [26]. The central government had, therefore, no incentive to record domestic trade in normal times. Neither the central government's system of Port Books, nor the local customs of ports like Chester or Southampton, can yield a body of information equivalent to that available for the foreign trades. But of all the internal trades, coastal shipping is the best-documented, and the deficiencies in our knowledge of even this sector underline the problems.

One of the principal strengths of the network of internal trading in sixteenth- and seventeenth-century England was the relative lightness of passage tolls, pontages, and other duties on domestic trade which created, in much of western Europe, a fairly rigid series of customs unions. Compared with France or Germany, England was a veritable free-trade area. But this real commercial strength leads directly to the historian's weakness: a lack of statistical information. Even the new corporations created in the seventeenth century and later to improve rivers and roads have left little material on actual trades [32; 28]. Thus it is that the historian of inland trade in this period has to rely on fragmentary and rather uncertain materials.

Subject to these warnings on the state of the available information, this chapter surveys the major trades of the period. Inevitably the account is biased towards the better-documented waterborne trades, and to coastal rather than inland traffic. With this in mind, sections (i) to (iii) discuss the cereal, livestock, and animal products trades, and the two concluding sections assess minerals and manufactures in rather less detail.

(i)

The matter of fundamental interest to Englishmen in our period, and, for that matter, long afterwards, was the state of the harvest.

13

It determined the needs for interregional and international cereal trades and, by its absorption of more or less of consumers' incomes, affected the sales of other commodities [74; 75; 77]. The higher grain prices resultant on bad harvests may have made transport costs more bearable and thus extended market areas.

It is not possible to establish the over-all pattern with satisfactory statistics, but, very broadly, our period saw a shift in the English cereal market from a position of marginal shortage *c.* 1500, to real deficiency in the mid- and late sixteenth century, and to substantial and growing surplus by the mid-seventeenth century. At both ends of the period there was an active export trade in grains, and this provides a means to assess regions of excess and deficiency, at least in crude terms. No equivalent figures are available for the bulk of the seventeenth century, but the results of this analysis of international shipments are presented in Table 1.

At best the data in Table 1 are rough guides to the regions of excess or deficiency. They suggest a fairly clear and unsurprising pattern of trade. The east coast dominated the export trades, and was followed by the west, which rather surprisingly made regular sales of corn abroad. Everitt regarded the south coast as the real second-ranked group of ports in cereal export in the period, and in the figures of Table 1 this area does look rather too small an exporter to be credible: the statistics for this group may be more than usually unreliable [35; 90]. In the north, the demands of the two headports were countervailing, Hull largely exporting, and the Newcastle group tending to import. London, of course, was a substantial importer, and came to depend on foreign imports of grain for its basic supply by the end of the sixteenth century. Part of the fluctuations visible in these figures can be attributed to unusual events, particularly to bad harvests, but it is still clear that a two-way international grain trade existed in the sixteenth century, and corns were even imported to King's Lynn [34]. While internal trade provided the supplies of wheat and barley for export, some return cargoes, probably of rye or oats, were made, and funnelled into home distribution.

This regional pattern of trade in corn is supported by the rather less substantial statistics for coastal shipments, presented in Table 2.

The east-coast ports were the dominant drains for corn, and inland trade routes fed Lynn, Boston, Yarmouth and Ipswich

TABLE 1

The International Grain Trade, 1500–1610

(Figures in quarters, annual averages, Michaelmas to Michaelmas)

Decade	North		East		London		South		West		Notional Balance
	In	Out	In	Out	In	Out	In	Out	In	Out	
1500–10	381	14	589	8821	3200	—	174	2098	988	3654	Positive
1510–20	1205	1032	280	4628	18271	—	104	1847	103	6092	Negative
1520–30	885	—	280	5908	—	—	—	884	87	5283	Positive
1530–40	—	—	140	9212	—	—	—	1525	302	276	Positive
1540–50	3764	260	—	15945	14488	—	—	—	217	2095	Negative
1550–60	341	—	930	1880	966	—	63	90	171	1136	Positive
1560–70	—	400	254	2886	—	—	—	421	590	2750	Positive
1570–80	—	1943	—	19429	—	1090	—	2345	—	654	Positive
1580–90	8918	1758	4710	22275	—	—	—	390	—	1415	Positive
1590–1600	—	—	1910	617	11028	—	—	—	65	—	Negative
1600–10	1888	—	—	5515	31596	144	—	790	2250	—	Negative

Figures are from Gras [34, appendixes B and C]. They are averages, by harvest years, of those years for which imports or exports are recorded, and do not indicate the real magnitudes of trade. They are guides to the net position of each group of ports and no more.

Imports for 1500–10 relate to those by aliens only.

Ports are grouped as follows: *North*, Hull to Newcastle headports; *East*, Thames to Lynn; *South*, Kent to Poole; *West*, Exeter to Bristol.

TABLE 2

Coastwise Shipments of Grain, 1540–1610

(Figures in quarters, annual averages, Michaelmas to Michaelmas)

Decade	North		East		London		South		West	
	In	Out	In	Out	In	Out	In	Out	In	Out
1540–50	15591	1073	—	40174	—	—	—	512	—	—
1550–60	4653	3499	—	19943	—	—	2601	10468	1972	2216
1560–70	11721	20	—	47165	324	615	—	15955	4765	903
1570–80	—	—	1355	26211	18090	195	—	—	—	2341
1580–90	1290	—	378	11828	51688	4926	—	185	762	364
1590–1600	—	—	—	14934	—	—	—	—	1910	572
1600–10	—	—	—	8098	—	—	—	874	—	—

Figures are averages of years or parts of years for which coastwise shipments are recorded, pooled into harvest years, and are taken from Gras [34, Appendix D]. As with the figures of Table 1, they represent no more than rough guides to the trading position of each group of ports. Port groupings are as in Table 1.
(Reproduced by permission of Harvard University Press.)

with a very large proportion of England's domestic grain shipped by coast. In these figures, southern ports assumed their expected significance, and the north, despite the exports of the Hull group, appears as a deficit region, largely because of the heavy imports of ports like Newcastle. Taken in the context of the international trade, western ports can be seen as entrepôts, importing on balance but sending substantial amounts of corn to Wales and Ireland. As in international trade, London was a vast consuming market, the focus for eastern and southern ports in normal years, but even the capital exported grains coastwise, confirming that the corn trade was supplied by regional specialisms which generated exchange.

The statistics are too defective for most of the seventeenth century to allow a similar approach. It seems likely that the export of corn abroad declined somewhat after 1600, but rose again and reached new levels in the second half of the century [35; 82]. Willan's work on the coasting trade suggests that the regional pattern of grain trade was much as in the sixteenth century, the absolute volume of corn rising substantially by 1700 [31]. East-coast ports like Yarmouth, Lynn and Ipswich continued to dominate the corn trades, although Hull and, by the 1730s, Berwick, increased their exports. Southern ports seem to have concentrated increasingly on the London market and the figures in Table 3 show the very considerable growth in the volume of shipments from Kent in the seventeenth century.

TABLE 3

Grain Shipments to London from Kentish Ports
(quarters)

1587–8	12,080	1649–50	44,980
1615	41,823	1675–6	17,088
1624	27,957	1680–1	71,090
1638	57,187	1699–1700	77,706

Figures from Chalklin [90, *175*].
(Reproduced by permission of Longman.)

During the century, Gloucester rose as a grain port, shipping to the Bristol entrepôt, and Bridgwater developed a trade in pulses to the same city, but few other developments of note took place in the western group. During the seventeenth century, then, the pattern of the late sixteenth century intensified, and the absolute volume of cereals shipped from the south and east coasts grew greatly.

It is less easy to decide what happened inland. Taking Gregory King's figures for the total output of corn in the 1690s, it is hard to attribute more than perhaps 5 per cent to recorded coasting or exporting trades [3, 782; 31]. Most of the leading corn-shipping ports were fed by major river systems, and their geographical advantages intensified during the seventeenth century as such rivers were 'improved' [32]. It would be an error to assume that seaborne traffic pointed exactly to directional flows of trade. The Thames, Lea, Wey and associated systems formed a massive source for London's barley and malt, even in the sixteenth century, and similar trades took place on most navigable rivers. Much of the grain carried on the Trent, the surplus of which was draining through Hull in 1700, probably never reached the coast. The major interregional and international trades used the sea, but represented a small part of total traffic. Much of the grain output of, say, the east midlands, which was swinging back from grass to corn after 1600, was distributed inland by road and river. As one would expect, the evidence of lawsuits from the Courts of Chancery and Requests adduced by Everitt, showed that three-quarters of grain transactions stemmed from eastern and southern England. The bulk of non-local trades in cereals were supplied from East Anglia, the east midlands, and from the vales, and later the downlands, of the south [35; 17; 18].

One final point needs to be made about the grain trade: corn was not a homogeneous commodity, and even individual grains exhibited a bewildering variety of qualities, types and prices. This is suggested by the two-way grain trades of both major importing ports, like London, and exporters, such as Lynn, and is confirmed by such glimpses as one can gain of the exact commodity structure of the cereal trade. Everitt found four-fifths of his lawsuits in the period 1500–1640 related to barley or malt, and a mere 13 per cent to wheat. Oats, rye, maslin, meal and legumes accounted for only 5 per cent of the total [35, 548]. By implication the English townsman of the period was supplied with barley bread. Figures of corn shipment from King's Lynn, Hull and Yarmouth for the seventeenth and the early eighteenth century confirm this view. These are presented in Table 4.

While by 1700 nearly 50,000 quarters of wheat and wheaten flour were being exported annually, double that quantity of malt and barley went abroad, and it was these latter two commodities that formed the staples of the domestic cereal trade [31; 24, *94f.*].

TABLE 4

Coastwise Trade of Lynn, Hull and Yarmouth, by Grains

(percentage of total)

	Barley/Malt	Wheat	Oats
King's Lynn			
1620–1	79·0	0·0	16·8
1734–5	61·2	4·9	25·1
Hull			
1627–8	60·0	18·7	21·3
1683–4	22·1	23·9	54·0
1731–2	4·2	39·6	56·2
Great Yarmouth			
1637–8	79·4	18·6	
1682–3	66·2	3·7	
1732–3	78·4	21·6	

Figures from Willan [31: *80–2*].
(Reproduced by permission of Manchester University Press.)

(ii)

Shipping records help to assess trades in animal products, but the basic livestock trades present greater problems. Apart from trade in cattle, sheep and pigs from Ireland, livestock trade by sea was unimportant in this period. Livestock trade was confined largely to the mainland of Great Britain. If figures of trade are lacking, for the year 1695 we do have Gregory King's estimates of livestock populations, and of annual consumption of meat. These figures, in Table 5, help to frame the analysis of these trades. While we have no real guides as to the accuracy of King's estimates, his outline of his methods and his vigorous defence of his figures in discussion with Robert Harley suggest that they are adequate to the present purpose [3, *797–8*]. The discussion of the livestock trades which follows is therefore based on King's figures for the end of the period.

Of these trades, that in cattle was the most valuable, and the supply of beeves to London the best-known. King's assumption of a static population of cattle suggests an annual consumption of 800,000 meat animals, comprising mature beeves and veals in the proportion of two to one. Assuming that King can be taken as a reasonable base, we can assess the significance of London's consumption in the late seventeenth century, and evaluate the contribution of the Celtic fringe to England's livestock supply. But it must be noted that King's own figures suggest a volume of total trade in cattle far greater than this: allowing for stores, well over a million head must have passed through English markets each year.

TABLE 5

Estimates of the Principal Livestock Herds, 1695

	Annual Increase/ Consumption	Total Stock	Value of Stock (net of skins) £
Beeves, stirks and calves	800,000	4,500,000	9,000,000
Sheep and lambs	3,200,000	11,000,000	4,400,000
Swine and pigs	1,300,000	2,000,000	1,600,000
Rabbits and conies	2,000,000	1,000,000	21,000
Horses and asses	100,000	1,200,000	3,000,000
Fowl	£ 620,000		460,000

Extracts from Gregory King, *Natural and Political Observations upon the State and Condition of England* (1695), printed in Thirsk and Cooper [3, 783].
(Reproduced by permission of the Oxford University Press.)

Many writers have emphasised the importance of the droving trades in cattle from Scotland and Wales in this period. It was reported that 18,574 cattle entered England through Carlisle in 1662, indicating that upwards of 30,000 head in all were driven across the border that year. By the 1680s, the volume of the trade was such that the exchange rate between London and Edinburgh was determined largely by the drovers. At the end of our period, between 1697 and 1703, Scots cattle paying English customs duties ranged between 11,000 and 60,000 each year [89, 212f.]. Three-quarters of this trade may have passed through Carlisle's toll jurisdiction, much coming from the major breeding area of Galloway, although some drove routes reached into the Highlands by 1700. Largely for political reasons, this trade must have been an innovation of the seventeenth century [40].

The Welsh droving trade was rather older, being traceable to the thirteenth century, but is more difficult to quantify. It had developed from the second quarter of the sixteenth century, growing in volume with the pacification of the borderland. From the fragmentary evidence available, it seems that Welsh trade may have run at about the peak of Scottish trade through the seventeenth century, or around 70,000 per annum. For the whole of our period Wales produced a significant proportion of England's beef, a share which rose to perhaps 1640, but tended to diminish thereafter [41; 42].

Added to the two mainland trades in the seventeenth century was the rapid growth of Irish cattle exports, which reached 50,000 per annum in the early 1660s, but which ceased as quickly with the final prohibition of trade in 1681 [43]. Putting all three cattle trades at their greatest, thus allowing generously for illicit or unrecorded traffic, the equivalent of up to one third of the annual slaughter of beeves (according to King's 1695 figures) was supplied from the Celtic fringe. Many of these beasts were stores, sold for fattening rather than for immediate consumption, and we must not exaggerate their direct effects on the English livestock market. If these imports equalled one quarter of total breed in volume, their share in value terms, as Scots commentators were swift to indicate, was considerably smaller. But even if the real profits on such beasts were made in England, the trades were of real significance to the supplying economy.

England's domestic producers supplied the bulk of all cattle passing through the market place, and the principal market lay in London. John Houghton collected opinions on the supply of cattle to the capital which allow some assessment of the flows of trade. Averaging the evidence of his 'ingenious butcher' and that of the horn trade (the raw material of combs, spectacle-rings, tobacco-boxes, fansticks, and a thousand other 'necessaries', according to Houghton), some 87,500 beeves, or 16·4 per cent of King's total trade, went to London. Of these, 35 per cent came from the north and north-west through Tottenham and Highgate; 23·5 per cent from the west, through St Giles; another 23·5 per cent northwards through Southwark; and 18 per cent from the east across Bow Bridge.[3] This pattern of trade extends Everitt's suggestion of a broadly south-easterly flow of cattle from the pastoral regions to 1700, although the fattening industries of East Anglia, the Thames-side marshlands and the southern counties were of more immediate importance to the capital. The regional specialisation which was already visible in 1500 was sustained and refined by the growth of an intricate network of drovers, graziers and butchers to 1700. The basic cattle trades ran from the north and west to the south and east, but were criss-crossed by local and regional currents. Despite the importance of the London market, and of supplies from Wales, Scotland and Ireland, the vast bulk of trade involved neither directly.

Less satisfactory evidence is available for other livestock trades. As with cattle, these are best approached on the basis of Table 5. Most numerous of all livestock in 1695 were the 11 million sheep and lambs. The annual breed, net of losses through disease, was put at 3·2 million, in exact balance with meat consumption. How can this be reconciled with the evidence on flocks at the beginning of our period? Perhaps the first surprise is that the sheep flock in 1695 may not have been any smaller than that of the early sixteenth century, when sheep were held to be the agents of depopulating enclosure. The problems of the early sixteenth century lay not so much in absolute numbers of sheep but in their type and geographical distribution. But changes in demand and output over the period made for substantial shifts in trading activity.

Gregory King's analysis of 1695 suggests a sheep population with an annual turnover of 30 per cent devoted largely to meat production. The implicit three-year fattening life for muttons seems acceptable, and these figures suggest a high level of trade. Assuming trades in lambs, breeding stocks and muttons, the number of animals passing through market places must have been as high as 4 millions each year. In contrast, the English sheep flock was devoted largely to wool production in the early sixteenth century. Large-scale sales of sheep did take place, but the trend, as Bowden showed, lay towards production on a greater scale, and its consequence was the growth of self-sustaining flocks. In the first half of the sixteenth century, then, turnover trade can be reduced to perhaps half the 1695 level, and this would put annual trade in sheep at around 2·5 million or less c. 1540 [36; 3, 783]. From the 1620s at least, the attraction of mutton-rearing was growing, and tended to throw more animals into the market place. Hence the two tendencies visible in the sheep trades were countervailing, and the decline in breeding-stock sales for wool output was met by the expansion of mutton consumption. All in all, the domestic trade in sheep and lambs must have grown considerably in the years 1500–1700, on these estimates by as much as 60 per cent.

Wales, Scotland and Ireland took a part in this trade. In terms of markets specialising in sheep, Wales stood on a level with the east region, the two providing about half the number of the midlands, or around 18 per cent of total. Evidence from the eighteenth century suggests that numbers of Welsh muttons traded across the border were growing in proportion to cattle, but it is uncertain whether this trend dated from the seventeenth century [40]. It has been held that Scotland contributed little to England's consumption of mutton or wool before 1700, but cross-border traffic did develop in the seventeenth century [40; 89]. Irish exports to England followed the same dramatic pattern as those of cattle, rising from 10,000 to 20,000 per annum in the later 1630s, to over 100,000, excluding Cumberland ports, in the 1660s, and reaching over 80,000 again in 1680 when the trade was briefly permitted once more [43]. But in the over-all context of an annual turnover of 3·2 million animals, yielding 10 million fleeces and fells in 1695, worth in all over £3·7 million, the contribution of such imports was negligible.

According to Houghton's informants, London was consuming 600,000 muttons a year in the 1690s, or around one sheep per head of population.[4] If correct, this indicated a level of consumption of mutton roughly 75 per cent greater than that of the rest of the country, when London's beef consumption was only 50 per cent more than that of the provinces. This represents a clear corrective to the standard histories of food, which underrate sheep as meat animals in the period [19]. More interesting is the implication that London acted as an entrepôt for mutton, the capital's consumption being artificially inflated by supplies passing through for export, military victualling or naval stores. There is little doubt in the sheep trades of the demand of the capital, which was increasingly felt in the period. As mixed farming methods diffused, the generality of countries must have produced some sheep for market, but, as in the cattle trades, the basic flow of the droving traffics ran from the north and west to the south and east. The apparently high density of sheep grazing in the home counties was as much a reflection of London's drawing power as of the natural suitability of their pastures [36; 91; 35].

After sheep the animal which sustained more industry and trade than any other was the horse. During this period it became generalised as a farm animal, but of the horse trade astonishingly little has been written, although in the records of fairs and markets it is better documented than that of most other commodities. Once more, King's estimates of population and turnover form our starting-point. These put the population of horses and asses as static at 1·2 million, with an annual breed of 100,000. Neither King nor his critic, Harley, attached any value to the horseflesh thus produced, and it seems unlikely that Englishmen in the sixteenth and seventeenth centuries, any more than their modern counterparts, thought of horses as potential dinners. Horses seem to have been considered as meat only in times of real dearth [19]. Horse trades therefore met only two basic demands: for draught and carting on the farm, and for draught and carriage in transport and trade.

This differentiation of demand led to a clear division of labour in the industry, in which breeding and rearing tended to be separate. In the latter trade, which supplied the final consumer, the midlands were dominant: the bulk of specialist horse markets in the period 1500–1640 lay in the midlands. The other principal trading centres lay on the borders of Essex, Suffolk and Cambridgeshire, in Shropshire and Herefordshire, and east Yorkshire. All of these were drawing at one remove from the specialist breeders located, on the whole, in the fens and forests. As markets, like the famous fair at Penkridge, had generally arisen on the fringes of rearing regions, their records suggest the dominance of local vendors. In so far as Warwick's horse sale records indicate a trade flow, the main receiving counties after Warwickshire were Gloucester, Somerset, Northampton and Oxford.[5] As in many of the livestock trades, the records of individual transactions suggest markets of limited extent.

Everitt's work supports this general conclusion. Interregional trade dealt largely with pack and riding-animals, and only rarely with farm horses, which were more commonly supplied by local breeders. Only the heaviest farm horses, for special markets, such as those from the vale of Taunton, crosses destined for the road-haulage industry, or the better riding-horses, warranted more distant trade in this period. The regional drifts that can be traced lay from the main breeding regions of Lincoln and Norfolk, the Somerset levels, Essex marshes, Cannock, the northern dales, and the forests of Pickering, Macclesfield, Northamptonshire, Arden and the New Forest, into the midlands and the eastern counties where schooling and rearing was founded on arable farming [17; 35]. Thereafter, perhaps not directly, horses tended to drift towards the capital, drawn by the demands of the transport trades, which, with pack-carriage and cartage, and riding-animals, accounted for perhaps half the total population.[6] Elsewhere, the growth of the north-eastern coalfield, and of mining in the west country, Wales and the borders, and the west midlands generated important and growing demands for both draught and pack animals. For all these final consumers, the dealers of the midlands, of south and east Yorkshire, and of the eastern counties, were the main suppliers.

Pigs were kept widely, and many studies of probate inventories reveal their presence, even in the lower strata of wealth. In the east and the midlands of England, perhaps half the labourers would have had a pig, even in towns where pigs fed on waste products came increasingly to represent a nuisance in the period. In contrast, pigs were relatively rare as cottage animals in the west and north of the country before 1640, where their ultimate diffusion was linked with that of the potato, largely after 1700 [17, 416]. King's estimate of 1·3 million pigs slaughtered each year shows bacon and pork as a basic element of diet in these centuries, but it is uncertain how many of these animals were subject to market transactions. Many labourers, and farmers like Robert Loder of Harwell, whose accounts survive for the years 1610–20, kept pigs and poultry purely for domestic consumption [7].

Bacon was, however, one of the few meats which could travel well and this, with other pig-based products like leather and soap, did find a place in the export trades of the major producing regions. Willan's studies of shipping reveal bacon being carried out of Hampshire and Dorset by sea, through Bristol from Somerset and Gloucestershire, from Cheshire and north Lancashire, and from Suffolk and Yorkshire [31; 35]. Wales and Cornwall were major breeding regions supplying fatteners in the west, and London for many producers was the principal market. Commercial pig-keeping remained grassland or forest-based before 1700, and tended to be a residual activity of dairymen or other pastoral farmers. Some exchanges of large herds revealed regional specialisms, and in Elizabethan England Hampshire was regarded as the producer of the best bacon, pigs being sent from Oxfordshire and Buckinghamshire to finish in its woodlands. But over all, pigmeat seems to have been rather more important in diet than in internal trade. While Gregory King's estimate of output in 1695 places the late seventeenth-century pig population just below the bottom point of the nineteenth-century pig cycle, trade in pigs and their meat was relatively smaller.

Similar problems arise with other livestock, such as rabbits or poultry: many were produced each year, far more perhaps than King allowed, but for the purely domestic consumption of farm, cottage or manor. Only a few areas seem to have engaged in substantial trades in such animals. East Anglia was most notable for its output of fowl, wild and domestic: the fens reared ducks, the poor sands were farmed for rabbits, and geese, hens and turkeys were kept in the cereal regions. Much of the poultry was driven overland to London, geese like cattle being shod for the journey, at the end of the harvest when roadside stubbles offered easy feeding [4, I, 59]. The number of markets which specialised in poultry and wildfowl was greatest in East Anglia, confirming this as the major producer, and after this only west Wales, by the same token, concentrated to any extent on the trade. According to King, these were more expensive meats, and would thus bear transport costs more easily, but represented a small part of total consumption by weight. But by underrating the importance of poultry, rabbits and game in the Englishman's diet, and overrating their value, King's figures give a misleading impression of the value of the trade. Such meats formed basic parts of cottage and farm diets, but were not a major commodity in the national market place. As with pigment, the value of poultry, game and rabbits as trade and as consumption goods diverged.

(iii)

Livestock also yielded an enormous range of products for both food consumption and manufacturing. The principal trades lay in leather, butter and cheese, wool, and, more locally, in milk and eggs. These commodities form our focus for the last section on trade in agricultural commodities.

The last two, milk and eggs, were confined more closely to the immediate locality of consumption, and represented largely the producers' responses to demand. London drew its milk from areas like Tottenham and other near-by parts of Middlesex, and was consuming nearly five million gallons in the early eighteenth century, a trade alone worth around £80,000 per annum. On a lesser scale, suburban producers supplied fresh milk to provincial towns, but the milk trade over all was a minor one. Neither the supplying capacity nor the dietary habit allowed the dairy industry to overcome the formidable barriers to its growth. Relatively little is known of the trade in eggs, though its smallness is perhaps indicated by the paucity of price material on the subject. None the less, by the later seventeenth century Scotland was an important supplier of eggs to England. Berwick saw considerable shipments of Scottish eggs in the 1680s, and over half a million were exported from Bo'ness in 1684/5 [89, 219]. Such trades seem to have been exceptional, and short-lived, declining rapidly after the 1680s. In general local and small-scale transactions characterised the egg trades.

First in importance, and certainly first in the volume of contemporary literature it generated, was the wool trade. Almost alone among the inland trades this already has its historian, and one need do little more than refer to Bowden's work here [36]. Most regions of the cloth industry were employing largely local supplies of wool, c. 1500, but as the industry expanded, and the export market for raw wools declined, the broadcloth regions looked increasingly to the wools of the west midlands for supplies, the old staples of exports. Gradual change in the nature of agriculture and of the woollen industries meant that supplies of suitable wools were wanting, and during the seventeenth century expanded interregional and import trades met the need. The trade in wools, and, to a much lesser extent, in yarns, was one of the great traffics of the period. If local supplies were adequate in 1500, by 1700 most of the great textile regions – the south-west, East Anglia, Yorkshire, Essex and Lancashire – needed to import wools or perhaps linen yarns, to continue business.

Such wools came largely from Lincolnshire, the midlands, or through London. As pastures and markets changed during the sixteenth century, long-stapled varieties of sheep diffused into the midlands, Ryder suggested from Lincolnshire, and the growth in this wool supply may have aided the development of worsteds in the west midlands in the subsequent century [39; 36]. Both supplies and markets for wools lay largely inland, and road not water carriage was the conventional mode of transport. Bowden's analysis of the industry suggested that even where easy access in shipping was to be had, at Exeter for example, road still seems to have been preferred [36]. Nevertheless, there was trade in wool and yarn by sea, and Yarmouth imported over 200 tons of yarn from London and Hull in 1733 [31, 93–4]. In all regions, London merchandising and distributive services played some part in the wool trades. To the extent that the principal manufactures came to need exogenous supplies of warp threads, or cheap yarns, inland trade in woollen products developed substantially over the seventeenth century. Throughout our period, as Bowden showed, the home trade in wools remained extensive, complex, and of fundamental importance to the English economy [36].

Butter and cheese were important items of diet, and the former also served some functions as industrial lubricant and detergent. Both commodities were in considerable demand for the provisioning of ships. Clearly much of the trade was based on sea-borne transport. As a consequence, some statistics exist to gauge the magnitude of London's supplies in the late seventeenth century, and these are presented in Table 6. These figures of London's supply exist almost in a vacuum, and may not be all that reliable. Cheese as a commodity was measured in differing ways, and there may be a considerable error term in the figures of Table 6.

But in default of better material, we can at least pick out the vital coastwise trade in butter from Yorkshire and the north-east, which was fostered by the developing salt industries of the region. An exchange trade in coal, salt and butter was visible in the north-east by the late seventeenth century [37; 31; 60]. Equally striking was the Suffolk dairying industry, which like the north-east was a greater supplier of butter than of cheese, which in Defoe's judgement was 'perhaps the worst in England' [4, 1, 53]. By contrast, the Cheshire cheese industry seems to have dominated London's supplies, being shipped by sea through Chester or Liverpool, or via the Trent through Hull. The two trades reveal a remarkable degree of specialisation and a heavy concentration by London merchant factors.

Two problems arise from what seems a simple and significant pattern. To what extent did the coastwise trade to London reflect over-all inland trade in butter and cheese, and how far back in time can this geographical pattern be pushed? First, it is clear that some cheese and butter was named generically and not specifically by place of origin: 'Cheshire Cheese' probably came from Lancashire, Shropshire and Derbyshire, in addition to its most obvious source [96; 38]. But the regional pattern of specialisation visible in the 1680s reflected largely natural advantages in terms of pastures, and for the same reason would have applied broadly to the mid-sixteenth century. But it would have applied in lesser degree, since from the 1550s the diversification in livestock farming, and shifts in patterns of demand, fostered the development of commercial dairying. Thus in the north-west, Yorkshire and Durham, Gloucestershire, Wilshire and Somerset, and parts of East Anglia, butter and cheese production were developing on a greater scale [37; 31; 18].

TABLE 6

Coastwise Shipments of Butter and Cheese to London, Christmas 1687 – Christmas 1688

Supplying Area	Butter		Cheese	
	Quantity (firkins)	Per cent	Quantity (Cheshire equiv.)	Per cent
N.-E. Coast	40,054	70·4	41,757	10·1
Suffolk	13,599	23·9	38,115	9·3
Norfolk	106	0·2	111	0·0
Lincs.	2,558	4·5	—	—
N.-W. Coast	—	—	330,973	80·4
Other	542·5	1·0	867	0·2
TOTAL	56,859·5	100·0	411,823	100·0

Based on McGrath [44, 230] and Zupko [25]. Butter firkins were officially standardised in 1662 at 56 lbs net of the barrel or 64 lbs gross. All cheeses have been taken as equivalent to Cheshire cheeses, and weight and volume measures converted accordingly at 224·5 cheeses to the ton. These are no more than rough guides to the volume of trade, particularly for cheese, where the official 10 lb. cheese is probably fictional [38].
(Reproduced by kind permission of Mr P. V. McGrath.)

It is therefore somewhat surprising to find relatively few of these known dairying regions featuring in London's seaborne supply in 1687–8. Superficially at least, our statistics look a little suspect. Gregory King's guesswork again assists the over-all assessment of the trade. King put the output of the dairying industry at £2·5 million in 1695, split in the proportion of 34, 48 and 18 per cent between butter, cheese, and milk and cream.[7] Using John Houghton's contemporary prices, it is possible to estimate total trades in butter and cheese. Trade in butter, c. 1695, was running at around 820,000 firkins, and in cheese at just under 10 millions of 'Cheshire equivalents'.[8] By volume, London received 6·9 per cent of butter marketed and 4·2 per cent of cheese coastwise. If we make the reasonable assumption that the capital consumed butter and cheese roughly in proportion to meat, 17·5 per cent of total produce should have been sent there for market. Thus only 40 per cent of its butter and 24 per cent of its cheese was recorded in our sample years as arriving by coastal shipping. This could be a quirk of the shipping statistics, but more likely reflects the great volume of Wiltshire, Gloucestershire and home-county butter and cheese, and the cheeses of Warwickshire and Leicestershire, which reached London by inland transport. Rough-and-ready arithmetic confirms Stern's assessment that London's basic supplies came inland, not coastwise, and suggests the real importance of inland trade in cheese [38]. Willan's comment that provincial coastwise trade in cheese was 'almost negligible' almost certainly undervalues Welsh output [17, *134–5*], but does further indicate that over all in the butter and cheese trades perhaps four-fifths of traffic was conducted inland, much, by implication, to relatively local markets.

As a craft industry, leather-working was widely distributed, the supply of its raw materials and the demand for its products being fairly generalised. None the less, some concentration took place in both the 'heavy' (tanned) and 'light' (dressed leather) trades. The former, which included shoemaking and tanning, were a number of distinct occupations linked by internal trade to an ultimate market, while the glovers and pursemakers of the 'light' sector were more integrated, purchasing raw materials and marketing finished products [61]. Despite this division, and the fragmented process structure of the 'heavy' sector, trade was based on local supplies of hides at the beginning of our period, and the association of the leather trade with centres of grazing regions – such as Coventry, Worcester, and Northampton – holds true to 1700. Even so the divisions in the industry were shown by trade as early as the 1570s, when Port Books recorded an exchange trade between Faversham and London in cured and raw hides [62].

As trades grew to 1700, such divisions of labour multiplied, and the growth of the livestock industry expanded the supply of raw material. By the late seventeenth century, the West Riding of Yorkshire had become an importer of raw hides; and as early as 1625 it was claimed that 5000 hides were being shipped there from London [62]. As a result of its great meat consumption, London was a key supplier of raw hide throughout the period, but was also a major importer of leather manufactures, such as Worcester's gloves. Despite the apparently plentiful supplies of skins produced domestically, both Ireland and Scotland exported to England throughout the period, though the latter trade declined through the seventeenth century as droving advanced and took with it the raw material which had produced an average of 500,000 hides for export each year from 1550 to 1625 [89, 217]. Clarkson has shown the leather industry to have been in relative decline after 1600, but trade in leathers, skins and leather manufactures seems to have grown and become more complex. King put the output of leather and skins at £2·4 million 1695, roughly equal to that of the dairying industry. Such had been the development of the division of labour in the industry that by the early eighteenth century the great leather market at Southwark offered leather ready cut, both upper and sole, by size, for the jobbing shoemakers [65, 217]. The leather trade indicates once more the growing importance of industry based on livestock products in this period, and the complexity of its organisation suggests the extent to which trading methods were being refined.

(iv)

After grain and woollens, traffic in minerals was the most important of the domestic trades in the period. These trades, especially in coal, grew considerably in both inland and coastwise carriage, and came to represent significant items of domestic exports by 1700. Consumption of minerals like coal, and of such products as iron goods, seems to have grown greatly in this period, a development which was sustained into the eighteenth century by rising real incomes [55; 56; 45].

The coal trades were the greatest, and are for the historian the most tantalising. Nef's statistics of the growth of output by regions offer answers to the questions we wish to ask, but prove of little real substance. But since no other synoptic work on the industry exists, Nef's estimates of growth are reproduced in Table 7.

TABLE 7

Estimated Annual Trade in Coal, by Water, in Tons, 1551–60 and 1681–90

	1551–60	1681–90
By sea, to east and south-west coasts of England	22,000	690,000
By sea, to Scotland	3,000	50,000
By sea, to west and south-west coasts of England, and Wales	4,000	80,000
By sea, to Ireland		60,000
By river, inland	10,000	250,000
TOTAL	39,000	1,130,000

Based on Nef [49, I, 179].

These figures overstate the extent of growth and may also under-rate the inland trade in coal, but can perhaps be taken as indicators of broad directional flows. The southern counties, centring on London, came to represent the principal domestic markets for coals, and these maritime shires were supplied from Newcastle and, towards the end of the seventeenth century, from Sunderland and Scotland. A better indicator of the real magnitude of growth in the coal trade can be found in the statistics of exports from Newcastle, from 1590 to 1709, in Table 8.

TABLE 8

Coastwise Shipment of Coal from Newcastle, 1590–1709
(Tonnage, Decadal Average)

1590–1600	120,343	1630–40	409,275	1670–80	489,458
1600–10	214,305	1640–50	——	1680–90	513,677
1610–20	206,661	1650–60	411,679	1690–1700	473,519
1620–30	296,794	1660–70	420,668	1700–9	489,463

Based on figures in Nef [49, II, Appendix D].

As indicated by the output of the premier coalfield, the rate of development of mineral trades was less dramatic than was suggested in Table 7, averaging around 4 per cent per annum. It seems unlikely that trade from other regions grew any faster, as Langton's work on the south-west Lancashire coalfield may suggest, and certainly none accounted for a greater tonnage of coastwise shipments [50]. Trades in coal clearly grew fast from small beginnings in the sixteenth century, and by 1700 had reached considerable proportions, largely on the basis of the Durham and Northumberland fields.

But in 1700, as in 1550, a very large part of the total output of the industry was traded and consumed locally. Something like one million tons, perhaps 40 per cent of output in 1700, were marketed inland, and this fact serves to correct the impression given by the Tyneside industry. Water carriage had much to do with the early development of north-eastern, Welsh and Scottish, Cumberland and Lancashire coal trades, and the western coalfields supplied the Bristol Channel area and Ireland by 1700. But local demand, local carriage, and local markets were the primary forces operating in most of the coalfields worked before 1700, including Yorkshire, the midlands, south-west Lancashire, and Kingswood Chase. By the 1690s, Warwickshire coals could compete in north Buckinghamshire with those imported through the rivers Thames and Ouse.[9] What was really striking to contemporaries about the north-eastern coal trade was its difference in nature as well as scale from that of the other colliery regions [49; 50; 16].

Although other trades in minerals developed or even began in the years 1500–1700, none were of quite the same significance, and coastal trade in all other minerals did not equal that in coal [31, *69*]. Of these, iron was the most important to the economy, and its significance rose during the period as new demands for weapons, tools and household goods were expressed. Iron grates, ovens and firedogs underpinned the expansion of the coal trades, although they accounted for but a small part of the total demand for iron wares. The iron industry changed profoundly between 1500 and 1700. From the late fifteenth century, the introduction and diffusion of the blast furnace changed the structure of the industry and with it that of the iron trade. It engendered the separation of smelting and manufacturing and the consequential linkages provided by domestic trade. Around 1600, such trades were running from the Wealden ports – Rye, Newhaven, Hastings and Pevensey – and through Bristol down the river Severn [52; 53].

Considerable change took place during the seventeenth century. The Wealden industry declined rapidly between 1620 and 1660, although it had recovered somewhat by 1700. New centres of production grew up, and by 1717, when a survey of ironworks was made, concentrations of furnaces existed in the Forest of Dean, Cheshire and north Staffordshire, south Yorkshire and Derbyshire, north Lancashire, Shropshire, and the Weald of Kent and Sussex [52]. Trade in furnace iron grew from around 19,000 tons per annum in the 1620s, to 23–24,000 tons in the 1650s, 20–21,000 in the 1680s, 23,000 by 1690, and perhaps 25,000 tons in the 1710s [51; 54]. But many manufacturing regions, such as the Birmingham plateau, Durham and south Wales, were deficient in supplies of tough pig iron, needed for the better quality manufactures, and some regions even lacked supplies of the 'coldshort' pig, the basic input to nailing and the poorer smithy trades. Interregional trade in bar and rod iron, and rarely in ores, by sea from Lancashire or Sussex through the Trent and the Severn met part of this demand. From there, large-scale 'putting-out' trades in rod for nailmakers took place in both south Yorkshire and the west midlands [53]. In addition, high-quality imports from the Baltic or earlier from Spain filled the gap [51; 54]. In the 1680s Ambrose Crowley moved from the midlands to Sunderland to take advantage of such supplies for his new slitting mills.[10] In the early eighteenth century, such imports averaged 16,700 tons a year [24, *140*]. By 1700, then, domestic trade in iron was running at around 40,000 tons per annum, representing an increase of 30 to 40 per cent over 1600. This iron fed the growing concentrations of iron manufacturing in south Staffordshire, Arden Warwickshire, south Yorkshire, and the north-east, as well as the generalised demand from smiths and farriers all over the country.

Of the non-ferrous metals, output of tin roughly doubled between 1500 and 1700, although production dipped significantly in the early seventeenth century as monopoly and other factors depressed trade. Tin revealed a relatively simple pattern of trade, largely from Devon and Cornwall to the London market, for manufacture and export, which gave rise to the dominance of the London merchants in the trade. Up to the mid-sixteenth century it was common for Devon tin pieces to be shipped to Southampton, and thence carried overland to London. Of the remainder of the industry's output (perhaps 40 per cent *c*. 1550 and 20 per cent *c.* 1700) not exported as either pieces or goods, pewter manufactures at towns like York, Bristol, Coventry and Norwich were the principal users, with the building industry generally, and specialised London trades such as organ-pipe manufacture, taking the residue. As in so many sectors of trade the capital played a dominant role [57; 58].

Extraction of copper and lead, and in the seventeenth century, zinc, produced similarly localised trades, which are rather less well documented than other metals. Both copper and zinc extraction were new industries in sixteenth-century England and, measured by export performance, remained small in 1700. In that year only 82 tons of wrought copper, and 87 tons of all kinds of brass were recorded in the export statistics [24, *164*]. But the latter industry engendered an extensive inland trade, which grew from the 1580s, since copper was mined in the south-west and in Cumberland, while calamine (for zinc) was produced mainly in Somerset, Gloucestershire, and Nottinghamshire. Keswick, Tintern and Nottinghamshire became the main areas of manufacture before 1690, and Bristol and Newcastle the principal ports for the trades in finished goods [59]. South Wales, particularly Neath, developed coal-based copper and lead smelting with imported ores [31, *177*]. Lead was an older trade, but still a limited one. Active mines lay in the Mendips, the Pennines and the Peak District, with more in Cardiganshire. Since lead was in use fairly generally, it had a national and an international market. Chester, Bristol and Aberdovey on the west coast, and Hull and Boston on the east, were the principal points of shipment, and, as in so many trades, London took the great majority of recorded coastal cargoes, many for re-export [31].

Salt and the trades in miscellaneous building-materials were the other important mineral traffics of the period. Salt was used for seasoning, but more significantly as an input to scores of trades, including butter, meat and fish. Despite the confusion created by monopoly patents in the later sixteenth century, output was confined to three regions throughout the period: the north-east coast, particularly Shields and Sunderland; the south coast, at Lymington; and inland in the Cheshire and Worcestershire 'wiches'. Bulk traffics were carried on sea and river, as late seventeenth-century excise cases reveal: lost cargoes were the occasion for repayment of tax, as when in 1705 Will Lyth, master of the *John* of Whitby, lost forty-two bushels of excised salt when wrecked on his way back from Sunderland.[11] Apart from general carriage to market, the basic movements in salt were to fishing ports or to entrepôts like Hull and Lynn, to ports dominant in the butter trade, such as Whitby, or as with other minerals to London. In the west, Gloucester was an important entrepôt for salt shipped down the Severn, and Liverpool also shipped salt after 1660. Bristol, the south-western fisheries and south Wales were the main recipients. Trade in salt tended to run coastwise, and the physical limits set by transport factors concentrated the salted fish, butter and meat trades near the coast, though the consequent trades in preserved foods were fairly generalised. Salt was an intermediate good in a complex pattern of commodity trades which developed rapidly from the mid-sixteenth century as technological changes and advances in the scale of the salt industry expanded output [31; 49; 60].

A vast quantity of miscellaneous goods can be traced in the records of the coastal trades, ranging from stone, slate, bricks and tiles, to pipeclay and copperas. Many of these, like some of the coal trades, were created by the general growth of interregional trade. Others, particularly stone trades, may not have stemmed from specific need or demand, but have been created by the demand for backcarriage and ballast in coasting. But reference to Willan's work on coastal shipping after 1600, or to local studies of individual ports, illustrates at once the great variety of minerals traded and the real difficulties in assessing prime movers in trade [31, 75–7].

(v)

Finally, a great volume of manufactures, craft products and, particularly from the 1550s [14; 15], imported goods, was moved around the country by tinker, pedlar or 'Manchester Man', and retailed through shop, market or fair. Many of these followed the trade routes established for commodity traffics. Cloths from Westmorland and Lancashire were carried overland to Southampton and London [26; 46], the latter being a great market for cloth where Blackwell Hall was the statutory market. Its records indicate the flows of trade through the seventeenth century and suggest that after growth to 1620, there was a depression between 1620 and 1650, growth being resumed after 1660 [48]. Through this function as a major entrepôt in the receipt of home products for export, through its own sizeable mercantile community, and through its conspicuous consumption, London was the dominant importer of wines, cloths and luxuries from abroad, and therefore the principal distributor for such goods in England [91–3]. As early as the 1580s, hops, spices and fine cloths marketed at Chester were received overland from London [95]. Over the country as a whole, such trades reciprocated with the many traffics in primary or semi-processed commodities which have been discussed extensively above. The incomes earned by the growing droving trades, the cereal traffics and other commerce provided the stimulus to these returns, made in the form of the trinkets and baubles which, to many contemporaries, filled England's overabundant import trade [14].

The bulk of manufactures were marketed at home by the inland trades, and, at least in 1500, the great majority of craft products were sent to local markets. Even in 1695, King estimated that four-fifths of domestic woollen products, by volume, were consumed at home.[12] Only exceptionally were products dependent upon seaborne commerce for more extensive markets. Outstanding as an example of this was the glass industry, which grew considerably from the 1560s in Newcastle, Gloucester, Bristol and London, and which achieved more extensive markets by coasting and river trades as productivity gains reduced prices in money terms [63; 64]. Even so, bottled goods, such as beers and spa waters, were being marketed fairly widely in England by 1700, often by land carriage. But these were unusual trades, and for the craftsmen manufacturing wooden platters, leather harness or woollen stockings markets generally lay nearer home, and trade was conducted overland [95].

There seems little point in attempting to catalogue these minor trades. They tended to follow the basic trade routes established in the commodity trades, since, at the simplest level, the two were exchanges. What can be said is that where some quantitative data exist, it appears that modest growth in the volume of trade of 2·5 to 3-fold can be traced in this period. Despite Nef's rather extravagant claims, it is difficult to document an increase of more than 400 per cent in the Newcastle coal trade between 1590 and 1700. But if the average pattern identified here was of slow growth, its consequences may have been greater. Its impact may have been disproportionately great in the transport trades, in mercantile institutions, and in the distributive trades. As in the cloth trade, the over-all pattern was made up of periods of growth and retardation. The mid-sixteenth century and the mid-seventeenth century both seem to have been characterised by depressed trade. Such growth in recorded commodity trades indicated considerable expansion of interregional trade, even in staple raw materials like wool, and by 1700 a complex and extensive home market was in existence. The growth in volume reflected and fostered an increasing division of labour, and helped to create such specialised manufacturing regions as the iron trades of Birmingham and south Yorkshire.

The description of basic trades above has suggested a pattern of development for the years 1500 to 1700, so far as our rather defective sources allow. The factors which permitted, encouraged or inhibited this development must now be assessed.

3   The Means of Trade

IT is clear that transport lay at the root of trading patterns in this period, and the contrasts exhibited by the livestock, the cereal and the mineral traffics, particularly before 1660, stemmed in part from their different degrees of dependence on land carriage. Transport facilities conditioned the market for all goods geographically, and even in 1776 Adam Smith was able to point to the most extensive markets as those served by water carriage. Around 1500, some commodities may have been limited in their markets by physical transport constraints, such as the inland glass industry, while most others faced price barriers to extensive sales. For all goods but those with negligible price elasticities of demand – at the beginning of the period probably only imported luxuries sold thus with 'money no object' – transport cost was a fundamental determinant of trade, and remained so to 1700. Transport services determined the extent of local monopoly, and the degree of perfection of the markets.

The history of sixteenth-century transport remains largely unwritten and, bar Willan's work on water carriage, little of substance exists for the seventeenth century. In this essential area of the subject the familiar problem of lack of information is combined with a paucity of academic interest. Despite these difficulties the attempt to analyse the structure of the transport system, and to assess the course of change in it, must be made if we are to comprehend internal trade in this period.

(i)

Although textbooks have tended to deprecate the quality, efficiency and importance of road transport in the early modern period, it was the basis of most trades, with the exception of some of the coastwise mineral traffics. The linkages between farm and market, between coal staithe and consumer, and between weaver and clothier, were all largely by road. Developments in the road-transport industry, and changes in the costs of carriage, underpinned the home market and contributed significantly to its development.

The bulk of local carriage was provided in 1500 by farmers or smallholders. Carts, pack-horses, and panniers slung on yokes over human shoulders were the basic means by which goods were conveyed to local markets, at least for the smaller producer or merchant. But it was the greater farmers who fed the more distant markets, and from the mid-sixteenth century probate inventories reveal the expansion of carting or carrying-facilities on the larger farms. From around the middle of the seventeenth century the four-wheeled farm wagon was diffusing through these classes, bringing with it the means of carrying cereals more efficiently to market. Some part of the gains from the buoyant prices and the structural changes of the 'Price Revolution' was channelled into investment in farming equipment. As such, these improved carts and wagons represented net additions to the capital stock of the transport industry [90, 107].

As early as the mid-fifteenth century, extensive systems of overland carriage, by cart, pack-horse and wain were being provided by carriers. Stephen Bateman carried cloths from Kendal to Southampton every year from 1492 to 1546 [26]. Two factors suggest that from the middle of the sixteenth century traffic was increasing significantly. In 1555, the first public and general statute to provide for the maintenance of highways was passed, its preface alluding to the 'noisome and tedious' road conditions resultant on the growth of traffic. At the same time, Stow suggested the year 1564, the long-wheelbase wagon with four wheels was introduced to public road-carrying. A larger and heavier version of the wagon which later spread to farms, it spread quickly in the next fifty years, as suggested by a proclamation of 1618 which attempted to curb its use. More clearly, its advantages were such that legal restraint was ineffectual [20; 22].

This growth continued during the seventeenth century. The larger stage wagon, with swivelling front axle, was introduced during this period, probably before 1650.[13] Recent estimates of the capacity of the carrying industry suggest that the output of scheduled services more than doubled between 1637 and 1715, and that their physical capacity grew proportionately. While it is unclear how far these developments affected purely provincial traffics, it is clear that real growth took place in the provision of transport services [27]. The public road-carrying industry significantly extended markets by bringing down time distances. It also improved its efficiency, the productivity gains from improved vehicles and organisation compounding the extension through cost reductions [21].

These changes were linked in a two-way relationship with roads, which may have responded to the challenges of growing traffics. We do not know how far the acts of 1555 and 1563, which established the repair of roads by parish labour, made for improved conditions, but clearly surfaces sufficient to allow growth in domestic trade were provided. But this growth in traffic in turn made parish repair inadequate to the new demands of heavy wagons, and by 1622 the first bill was introduced seeking turnpike toll finance of repairs. From the 1660s, turnpike roads spread, and by the 1750s England's trunk roads were largely turnpiked [28]. This applied little to our period, but was symptomatic of the growth of demand for road improvement in the seventeenth century, which before 1700 was expressed in terms of bridge works on a considerable scale [21; 80]. While the real qualitative improvement of roads had to wait until the eighteenth century, it is clear that the stimulus to action lay in the growth of demand with which established institutions like the parish were unable to cope.

These changes physically extended the potential markets for goods, and allowed faster and cheaper passenger carriage and posting. The great innovation of the seventeenth century, the stagecoach, widened the range of commercial information and business opportunity in the hands of traders and producers [21]. Through such changes, the speed with which information travelled was significantly advanced, and it is clear from the correspondence books of landed estates that such information was used in making marketing decisions, especially in the livestock trades. By imitation, and through local gossip, these decisions permeated downward to middling farmers who, as transport facilities were improved, were increasingly able to take advantage of them. Such were the means through which the efficiency of the home market was advanced.

(ii)

Whatever the magnitude of the growth in the effective capacity of the road transport industry between 1500 and 1700 – it may have grown by at least three- or four-fold in the period – its market generally lay outside the mineral and the lesser cereal trades in which, given the low value by volume carried, lower carriage rates were essential. While there was some overlap between land and water carriage, as Willan's work showed, it is important not to assume that the demand for transport services was homogeneous. As our earlier study of the profile of trades showed, cart and wagon, and trow and hoy tended to serve rather different functions.

Carriage of goods on rivers had very considerable cost advantages over land carriage, measured simply by prices per ton mile, and real improvements were made in river navigation in this period. A mixture of the demand of interregional trade, the urge to redress local imbalances of supply, or, in the sixteenth century, to control flooding, motivated the 'improvers'. Although the major moves to improve rivers stemmed only from the 1660s, the technological, propagandist and economic history reached further back. Mixed but effective motives in the sixteenth century had produced the Exeter Canal, with its pound locks (1564), and the improvement of the Lea (1570s) [32]. Before the Civil War such motives, aided by the availability of royal Letters Patent, generated attempts to 'improve' the Warwickshire Avon, the Bristol Avon, the Tone and the Lark, although not all succeeded [32; 33]. While real investment, protected by act of parliament, was concentrated in the later seventeenth century, many of the needs, the entrepreneurship and the skills were available by 1650 [32].

How did such developments aid the cause of home trade? In a simple way, they were a substantial part of it. Transport services and engineering works contributed to employment, and their growth contributed to the demand for agricultural goods [6]. Navigable inland waterways grew from 685 miles in 1600–60 to 960 miles c. 1700, and to 1160 miles by 1730 [32], although Ward has recently suggested that some of these gains were illusory [33]. Willan's work did not extend back to the sixteenth century, but it seems likely that as much as a tenth of the mileage of navigable river available in 1600–60 had been ensured by the work of individuals or Commissions of Sewers before 1600 [80].

In terms of cost and economic impact, it is possible to be more precise. In absolute terms, river transport enjoyed a greater cost advantage than was normally expressed in the market, since tolls and monopoly rights were the normal, and perhaps proper, rewards for the owners of riparian rights. Road carriers were largely unaffected by such costs. Over the modal journey for cereals suggested by Everitt, 35–40 miles or less, this cost advantage was of the order of two-thirds, reduced to perhaps half by these restrictive practices [35; 32]. Thus, for the areas which benefited, the effective market area may have doubled, and it is clear that by 1700 good use was being made of some of these navigations. It has been estimated that in 1732 the Yorkshire Ouse was carrying over 20,000 tons per annum, and the growth in trade as a result of the Wye navigation in Hereford was such that the formal markets broke down [70].

To the extent that transport costs were reduced, river improvement extended markets in sixteenth- and seventeenth-century England. The actual extent of improvement appears small, although it did provide water transport in landlocked regions. Such penetration was probably more than proportionate in its savings, and the trading potential thus released had clear multiplier effects both on the transport industry and on the regional economies involved. Taken with technical changes on existing waterways, such as improved barges and pound-locking, which spread after 1550, it seems possible that the effective capacity of England's inland waterways more than doubled by 1700. In this it at least equalled the lower bound of the expansion of total domestic trade.

(iii)

Seventeenth-century Englishmen tended to regard the coasting trade as an extension of the river system, which in some trades it undoubtedly was. Vessels from the rivers of eastern England were probably capable of sailing coastwise to London without transhipping their cargoes of grain, at least in the second half of the seventeenth century. As discussed above, there exist for the study of the coasting trade some statistical sources which we lack for other carriage, and, as a result, historians may have exaggerated its importance in the total supply of transport services. As in river trade the comparative advantage of coastal shipping was expressed most clearly in the carriage of low-value/high-bulk commodities, such as coal and grain, and not typically in the transport of cloths, wools and manufactures, although many examples of the carriage of such goods can be found [31]. Two major issues therefore arise in the assessment of the industry: what was the extent of coastal shipping capacity in the sixteenth and seventeenth centuries; and what was the nature of its markets?

Statistics are available for the growth of total tonnages in shipping from 1560 to 1702, but undifferentiated by function. After some development in the early sixteenth century, shipping stagnated or declined in mid-century, and the 1560 estimate in Table 9 represents the position shortly after this nadir in merchant shipping.

TABLE 9
Estimates of English Merchant Shipping, 1560–1702
(tons burden)

1560	c. 50,000	1629	115,000
1572	50,000	1686	340,000
1582	67,000	1702	323,000

From Davis [30, 7–15].
(Reproduced by kind permission of Prof. R. Davis.)

Sadly, we cannot be certain how much of this tonnage was employed in coasting, nor what percentage of output of shipping services was represented by English shipping. Willan suggested that provincially-owned coastal shipping accounted for a quarter of total tonnage at the beginning of the eighteenth century, and Davies has suggested that half of total shipping in the mid-seventeenth century was employed in coasting or fishing [30, 16]. L. A. Harper's breakdown of the tonnage by trades is questionable, but offers the chance to assess the coasting trade over much of our period. Table 10 is based on Harper's estimates.

Harper's figures are only rough guides to the volume of growth in the period, but it is clear that the coal industry led to very substantial expansion in the coasting trade in the seventeenth century. But at least to the 1650s, alien ships, principally Dutch, penetrated the coasting trade, and their contribution to capacity must be allowed for. Thus the index of coasting in Table 10, which makes this allowance, suggests a curve of growth which is somewhat easier to reconcile with the evidence of cargoes carried. If Harper's figures probably overstate the size of the fleet in 1609–15, and understate in 1660 [30], it still seems clear that growth was concentrated into the later sixteenth and the later seventeenth centuries.

To this growth must be added the gains of the probable

increases in the efficiency of the industry, in which improved naval architecture permitted improved turn-round times, but more significantly, reduced crewing and victualling costs [30]. The shipping cost of sending coal from Hull to London was 8s. a ton in 1605. By 1670, the rate from Newcastle to London had dropped to about 4s. 7½d., and it fell to around 2s. 3½d. per ton in 1703. As in the river trades, restrictive practices and monopolies prevented the full transmission of these productivity gains to the consumer. None the less, such cost reductions, if representative of the trade as a whole, more than offset the reduced contribution of foreign coasters in the second half of the seventeenth century [31].

TABLE 10

Estimated Distribution of English Tonnage, 1582–1702

	1582	1609–15	1660	1702
Coal	7,618	28,223	70,899	78,212
Fishing	17,316	27,721	23,489	24,920
Coasting	10,607	15,743	25,021	41,454
Index of Total Coasting (1582 = 100)	100	196	226	357

Based on Harper [81]. The index of total coasting excludes the 'Coal' tonnage, and allows for the contribution of alien shipping to the total domestic supply, as follows: *1582* + 15 per cent; *1609–15*, + 25 per cent; *1660*, + 10 per cent; *1702*, + 5 per cent. Harper's figures are assessed fully in Davis [30].
(Reproduced by kind permission of Prof. L. A. Harper and Columbia University Press.)

Such gains did not apply as forcibly in the west-coast trades, in which smaller vessels predominated, but there is no real doubt that the capacity of the coasting trade grew at least threefold between 1580 and 1700. As this growth occurred, prices fell and created further trading potential. Such gains were offset by restrictive practices and by seasonal factors. The coasting trade was reduced to small proportions in January and February [77,5]. Risks were also greater than with river and road traffic, and losses through damage, delay, pilfering by man or rat, or, up to the middle of the seventeenth century, piracy, added to the real price of seaborne traffic. Such factors made coastwise shipping uneconomic for many traffics from London to the north-west [95].

Apart from the major shippers in the east-coast trades, actual output may have been rather lower than the growth in capacity suggested. It was thought that coasters could achieve ten or twelve voyages a year in 1738, but observations of shipping cleared in the Port Books suggest that the normal output was much lower, many of the smaller ships making no more than one or two voyages a year [31]. This fact may serve as a double warning of the deficiencies of the Port Books as records of coastwise trade, and of the gains in output made by the coastal shipping industry in the period 1582–1702.

(iv)

The transport industry made considerable advances in the period from 1500 to 1700, and contributed very substantially to the growth in domestic trade. The output of services on land and around the coasts more than doubled in the seventeenth century, and river navigations added to the market potential of midland and western parts even before 1660. Additionally, from the middle of the seventeenth century, wagonways were being laid down in the north-east coalfield to provide cheaper and easier access to the coast [29]. As the capacity and the output of transport services grew, the price of carriage experienced a secular fall, perhaps by 50 per cent in money terms and by rather more in the coasting trades. Improved productivity, greater speed and reliability, and the gains from scale in service networks were the vital components of this growth. The improved overland communications aided the dissemination of commercial information, and thus contributed to the growing efficiency of markets. While we cannot as yet gauge the exact extent of advances in transport before 1550, it is clear that over the two centuries from 1500 the means of trade at the disposal of merchants and producers were very substantially increased. What use they made of these facilities must now be considered.

4   The Conduct of Trade

INLAND trade varied as greatly in its conduct as in its means. There was an established system of regulated trading, in the markets and fairs created from the middle ages, and in these the activities of wholesale traders were carefully limited. But the reality of internal trading diverged from the regulated structure. In one sense, to examine the conduct of trade is merely to follow the logical consequences of the changing transport structure, but in another it provides a tool with which to assess the origins of the urge to improve means of carriage.

Sadly, relatively little direct evidence exists of the market strategies of producers and merchants, although some analysis of mercantile behaviour is possible on the basis of entries in the Port Books. Nor, since few documents survive, can certain conclusions be drawn on the nature of commercial information exchanged between traders, and on the exact means of account adopted in internal trading. The middleman has been seen by Westerfield and others as a key element in the development of the English economy before the Industrial Revolution, and his role in internal trade must therefore be assessed, despite the unsatisfactory nature of the available evidence. The issues of market strategies, the structure of commercial information, and of methods of account are the concern of the present chapter.

(i)

The two marketing institutions available to legal traders were the market and the fair. The two were distinguished by the time at which they were held and, perhaps in part consequentially, by the commodities traded within them. As Everitt demonstrated, the official system was neither complete nor unchanging at the end of the fifteenth century, and the sixteenth and seventeenth centuries saw the grant of new markets and fairs in many parts of the country [35]. But both institutions came under pressure from illicit, but increasingly effective, private markets at the same time. As some markets prospered on the basis of this growing trade, others stagnated, many declined, and some disappeared. What does this process suggest of the conduct of inland trade?

England and Wales had some eight hundred market towns before 1640, slightly fewer than half the peak reached during the expansion of the high middle ages. Their spatial distribution was such that the cereal regions supported a greater density than the pastoral: Wales had one market per 100,000 acres, the north one to over 80,000, while the south-west and the midlands had one to every 35,000 [35, *496f.*]. By adding the dimension of time, this spacing was substantially widened. In Berkshire, in the seventeenth century, only two towns held markets on the same day within twenty miles of each other. During the seventeenth century, this spacing between markets was being extended. In the west country, where market towns had been thickly strewn by medieval plantation, the century saw a considerable 'shake-out' of markets regarded by merchants as real. By 1700, Devon's 45 market towns had fallen in real terms to 27, and dropped to 20 by 1720; Somerset lost 9 and Gloucestershire 8 in the same period [70]. Numbers did not actually reduce *de jure*, but the expression of commercial forces increasingly distinguished the real from the notional trading place for all but local transactions. Trade began to concentrate in favoured centres and, in so doing, created the 'lost markets' which came to parallel the lost village of earlier times.

The seasonal marketing function, often outside the confines of towns, was served by the fair. Despite Westerfield's view that this institution declined in this period, the evidence of such almanacs as the *British Merlin* suggests that numbers may have grown, and there were 7 per cent more fairs recorded for England in 1750 than in 1660. Analysis of similar material provides a clear seasonal pattern. Over all, the number of days provided for trading in fairs peaked in May, with October, April and September following. The distribution was therefore around a major spring peak and a lesser one in the autumn. This pattern suggests that the fair's essential function lay in the livestock trades. The average distribution of fair days is best explained by springtime sales of stock, stores, and of animal products like wool, with post-harvest sales of consumer goods, such as clothes, explaining the autumnal peak. That fair trade was specific to agricultural fluctuations is suggested by the fact that different countries displayed differing seasonal patterns: Shropshire's peak occurred in

May, reflecting its pastoral strength, while Hampshire's greater interest in cereal farming was signified by its peak in October. But not all fairs were of equal commercial weight, and the many which came to be mere social events, characterised by 'drolls' and 'poppit shows', may rehabilitate some of Westerfield's criticisms. As with the plantation of new markets, the growth in the absolute number of fairs may disguise a real fall in their significance.

Several alternatives grew up to supplant these ancient institutions, although our period saw but the early parts of the process: the shake-out of the feebler markets and fairs was a long-term process finally accelerated by the canals and the railways. For the retail trades, small local transactions remained largely in the open market until late in the eighteenth century. Historians conventionally date the growth of the shop in the food trades very late, rarely before 1800, although most occupational evidence suggests that shops of many kinds were already widely dispersed by 1700, even outside the larger towns [66; 67; 68]. In the food trades, hawking and peddling were early developments, and, with the Manchester men and others who travelled the roads of sixteenth- and seventeenth-century England selling cloths, craft wares and other consumer goods, provided retail outlets of growing importance in our period. These were, in the long term, the substitutes for the open retail market.

Neither reached maturity as a threat before 1700, outside the pages of propagandist literature [3, *389f.*]. More serious a source of the decline of 'real' markets and fairs was the growth of private marts outside the confines of the town square, and of the direct trade of middleman with producer. Both seem to have developed very substantially in this period, as functions of the spread of the major interregional trades in agricultural commodities [35]. Inns, or their yards, were common if not normal resorts of private markets, and their many facilities served further to attract the merchant factors to whom these private, quasi-wholesale, markets were of the greatest service [69]. At the same time, fluctuations in market prices and sixteenth-century conditions of dearth may have aided the pre-contracted sales by farmers to those scourges of the commonweal, the forestallers. Growing non-agrarian populations, like that of London, demanded wider regions of supply, and facilitated the growth of middleman factors who, like the farmers with whom they dealt, sought certainty of supply and price. By the late seventeenth century such connections were commonplace and were growing. Defoe even suggested that the growth of private sales by sample facilitated these illicit links between producers and factors. Once commercial links had been forged in an inn between farmer and middleman, he suggested, the two would abandon trade in the market town altogether, in favour of direct sale, often of corn in the ground [6, II, *181*].

Both formal institutions of marketing were thus under growing threat in this period from more 'modern' and efficient systems. If, as yet, the extent of this competition cannot be defined, the growing magnitude of its effects can be traced. The open market of medieval England was far less relevant to the needs of the economy in 1700, and the fair, while basic to the needs of the livestock trades, both local and regional, may have been entering a prolonged period of decline [35; 70].

(ii)

The principal agents of that decline, contemporaries agreed, were the middlemen and factors. Such men appeared regularly in lawsuits, and still more frequently in the literature of complaint in this period, but very little is known about individuals. They exist more clearly in their actual or alleged consequences than as independent historical figures. It is important to understand the nature and development of this mercantile sector to be able to assess the causation of revealed changes in markets and trades. But as in many areas of this subject, a survey of existing literature leads to an appeal for more basic research.

R. B. Westerfield's work of over sixty years ago remains the only work on the middleman of the period, and his broad thesis of a considerable growth in the number, specialism and significance of middlemen in business in the century after 1660 remains largely unaltered by subsequent research [65]. Their economic function was clear: they formed the links in the market network, as in the Lancashire textile industry, and hence fostered specialisation [46; 47]. The growth in the numbers of trading factors, and the competition between them, helped to reduce transit costs, and thus by cost-reductions to extend markets further. The growth both of the class as a whole, and of the degree of their specialisms, hence aided the development of the domestic trades.

Some examination of individuals may help us to see how far back beyond 1660 this analysis can be pushed. Port Books record shippers as well as commodities shipped, in theory if not always in practice, and studies of coastal shipping help greatly in this study of the articulation of the domestic market. Willan's studies suggested that the medium-sized enterprise of the general merchant typified the coasting trade after 1600, although Woodward's studies of the Irish cattle trades suggest exceptions [43]. Butchers controlled much of the Dublin cattle trade to the northwest in the 1660s, and the exploitation of the consumer, the docker and the retailer by the larger factors in the east-coast coal trade was notorious [49]. But in such trades, masters still served as merchants in 1700, and throughout the period it was normal for shippers to serve also as shipowners. In some trades, such as corn and cheese, London merchant houses of greater scale developed, and by the end of the seventeenth century commonly employed their own factors at the port of supply. London corn-factors had provincial agents for their sales to Liverpool and Warrington by at least the mid-seventeenth century, and probably earlier [37; 38].

The nature of overland trade is less easy to assess. Early in the period one can find evidence of individual middlemen seeking out supplies for more distant markets. The men of Yaxley, Huntingdonshire, accused Thomas Aylward of Lynn of carrying away peas to Scotland in 1528, as a result of which 'pyned vs for hungger here', and objected to his attempt to do likewise in 1529 [1, I, 144]. Factors continued to gather their own supplies in this manner throughout the period, since the inland trades may have dealt, as a rule, in smaller quantities of supplies than the coastal merchants. Substantial men existed in the cattle trades, but not as commonly in the primary droving business: neither Hughes nor Haldane suggests larger-scale middleman enterprises at this level. John Griffith, a Welsh drover, expended over £4,000 on cattle in 1693–4, many of which he sold in England, but as the subsequent litigation proved, the bulk of the capital was provided by David Williams Esq., the grazier.[14] As Westerfield suggested, the greater factors were concentrated nearer the point of ultimate consumption, as graziers or jobbers. One of the greatest of such men was William Porey of Lincolnshire, who was employed by the inhabitants of the Parts of Holland in 1637 to supply an annual charge of 200 fat muttons and 20 fat oxen to the royal household, and who defaulted on his contract (worth £350) when he was bankrupted in exchange dealings with Ireland in 1640.[15] Another lawsuit, from 1698, indicated that John Loach had reneged on his partnership with Sam. Blanchard, cabinet-maker and citizen of London, taking advantage of the latter's extensive network of agents in Gloucestershire and Monmouth, and thus poaching supplies of walnut and fine woods.[16] The specific evidence tends therefore to support the view that an extensive network of middleman merchants was in existence in this period. But, as in the shipping business, the development of semi-formal agencies for major factors was a later development, documented most clearly in the later seventeenth century.

For all the specific trades delineated by Westerfield, in 1700, as in 1500, many of the middling factors who comprised the backbone of the inland trade were generalists, men who dealt largely on their own account in whatever was going. There were, of course, exceptions, such as the Hostmen of Newcastle who dominated the coal trade, or the Blackwell Hall factors who controlled the London cloth markets, but smaller middlemen were less able to concentrate [65]. The real gains of the sixteenth and seventeenth centuries were in their number, distribution and interconnection. The articulation of home markets took place on the basis of a very substantial growth in what Westerfield called 'the commercial population', not, as yet, through the creation of mercantile empires in the inland trades.

(iii)

Part, at least, of the growth in economic activity in the home market in the sixteenth century can be attributed to the growth in the money supply, although the relationship between the two was complex and has yet to be defined satisfactorily. The early growth of the textile industry and of the wool trade generated considerable demands for money, and domestic trade must take its place among the 'real' factors in the Price Revolution to which historians have accorded so much weight of late [71].

But one of the most important features of inland trade in the sixteenth and seventeenth centuries was its extensive and growing use of credit. Postan drew attention long ago to the importance of trade credit in medieval society, pointing out that 'sale credits . . . in reality formed the basis of medieval trade' [78, 87].

The growth of such credit mechanisms, and others, in the two centuries after 1500 may have had much to do with the growth in the absolute volume of that trade, and the diffusion of credit downwards to the lesser producers and traders added significantly to that growth.

Several features of the inland trades of this period point to just such an expansion of credit mechanisms – the effective growth of the money supply for transaction demands. Probate inventories, required for all testators with movable wealth over £5 in value – effectively the bulk of the lesser commercial classes – provide considerable evidence of small credits and larger loan bonds at many levels. Even in villages like Chippenham (Cambridgeshire) and Myddle (Shropshire) credit appeared widespread in the seventeenth century [96; 97]. Further up the commercial scale, credit was the foundation of the domestic wool trade, the coal and mineral trades, and many others, larger transactions being secured by conditional bonds. From the second half of the sixteenth century onwards, the principal courts – Requests, Exchequer, and Chancery – were full of the complex lawsuits resultant on such bonds, either through default or, like the case of William Porey in 1640, through the progressive collapse of an extended credit mechanism. By the end of the seventeenth century, Defoe was able to advise young tradesmen to secure their credit above all, since that alone was the essential base of trade [6].

Sale credits and the like were widespread in our period, and grew in parallel with trade. The decline of canonical sanctions against usury after the 1540s, and what has been called the 'silver revolution' in the English currency between 1520 and 1680, aided the extension of such credit networks [71, 51]. In the seventeenth century, the growth of primitive banking agents, such as goldsmiths, lawyers and scriveners, furthered this development. Such men acted as the ultimate discounters for the large and growing numbers of bills which circulated in seventeenth-century England. When, a little after the end of our period, Richard Stacey, keeper of the Swan Inn, Felstead, Essex, died, he held some eleven such bills and promissory notes from local and London tradesmen.[17] Only the vagaries of survival prevent a broad base of similar material being discovered for the second half of the seventeenth century, or earlier.

Other developments, principally in loan finance, further aided the refinement of the trading economy. Although the larger land-mortgage market did not mature until the later seventeenth century, loans, as opposed to sale credits and deferred payments, entered inland trade increasingly from the middle of the sixteenth century [79; 79a]. As the intensive study of inventories has shown, traders were probably able to meet short-run liquidity crises from local sources. At such a level, credit, even without interest, met the pressing needs of village and town dowagers and retiring yeomen for secure repositories for funds. Thus tradesmen of many kinds, such as innkeepers, drew capital into domestic trade through small mortgages, rent charges and loans. William Stout, grocer of Lancaster, borrowed at interest to advance himself in his trade, and suffered losses in 1730 when a fellow tradesman, Thomas Fox, the Kendal to Preston carrier, was bankrupted [9, 205]. As early as 1681 his fellow Quakers had been accused of favouring their co-religionists through extended credit networks, 'selling to all the world but buying only from their own tribe' [3, 394]. In truth, credit to start or advance commercial capitals, and to satisfy the need of the potential rentier, was less limited. To what extent it was generalised is as yet unknown, but the evidence of such studies as are at present available suggests that loan finance must be added to our analysis of the developing means of trade in the period. As far back as the early probate inventories of the mid-sixteenth century, loan transactions are visible in the middle ranks of English commercial society, and it seems clear that this facility developed to 1700. No less than trade credit, then, can money-lending be omitted from the over-all analysis.

Two forms of credit have been discussed here. Bowden's detailed study of the wool trade remains the only complete assessment of the part played by such credits in commerce, but his stress on its significance can clearly be extended to inland trade in general. From 1550 to 1700 at least, both sale and loan credits, the latter at a secularly-falling price, seem to have helped to underpin the growth in trades. In the words of that great propagandist for the home trades, Daniel Defoe, credit to the tradesman was as 'marrow to his bones' [6, II, 156].

(iv)

One final aspect of the conduct of trade in the period lay in the level of commercial awareness and in the access of the factors to valid information. Westerfield argued that it was the very existence of separate local markets, and the imperfection of the transmission of commercial information between them which sustained the growth of the intricate network of middlemen between 1660 and 1760. John followed him in seeing the extension of knowledge of the state of markets through the development of newspapers and transport as key elements in the advance of the home market prior to industrialisation [45]. Both scholars stressed the importance of such changes to eighteenth-century developments, but there are reasons to think that the process of change stretched further back in time.

As we have seen, communications were much improved in our period, especially after 1550. Shipping and coastal shipping, with river navigations and road-carriers all helped extend the bounds of markets by acting on costs. The advance of postal services, publishing and passenger transport all helped the integration of domestic markets, and made the information base for the expansion of middleman operations. Most of these advances were concentrated after 1600. Road-transport facilities for passengers developed from the simple riding-horses available *c.* 1600, to a few regular stagecoach services from provincial centres to London in 1637, and by 1715 such coach services to London had reached over 900 each week, and served every region of the country.[18] In absolute terms, the speed of travel had not increased very much at its fastest, and the fastest posts could transmit news quite rapidly. But costs of posting and riding by post-horse were high in the sixteenth century. The new services permitted cheaper carriage of the traveller, and easier communication between factors and their agents. Despite reform, the Post Office was unable to offer a comprehensive service after 1660, and the supplementation of postal services provided by unofficial carriers was crucial to the expansion of total communications. The second half of the seventeenth century thus saw a real expansion in the potential means for the exchange of commercial information. Was it used?

The question is as yet unanswered. That farmers and middleman factors discriminated between markets was undoubtedly the case, and the first literary remains from producers like Henry Best confirm the evidence of the differential performance of markets and fairs. Best may have been exceptional in his practice, but he distinguished between summer and winter market regions, and between cereal and cattle marts, but his records of the early 1640s do not suggest the kind of growth in market information which is clear in the evidence of the later seventeenth century [8]. In the later seventeenth century one begins to find heightening awareness among estate stewards, but little of substance to confirm the external evidence of the growth of the 'media'. If the market basis for John Houghton's periodical *Collection for the Improvement of Husbandry and Trade* of the 1690s was laid in the half-century from 1650, then it is exceptionally difficult to document it. The work of Granger and Elliott suggests that such factors had operated to the extent that by the second quarter of the eighteenth century the domestic market in wheat was broadly integrated [73]. This trend fits well with the evidence of the advance of information networks from the middle of the seventeenth century, but is no more than an association: the connection has not yet been demonstrated satisfactorily. But we can, none the less, draw the conclusion that the commercial information structure of England in 1700 was much improved by comparison with 1500, even if the pace of its improvement had been moderate until the mid-seventeenth century. Its full impact may well have been delayed until the early eighteenth century.

(v)

Even in 1500 the conduct of domestic trade was far from being a simple matter of the exchanges in open markets of goods for specie. Credit was already established as a means of trade, and its use grew very substantially in the next two centuries. The regulated trading system of markets and fairs seems to have been challenged by various influences of middlemen factors, expressed through 'forestalling' or private marketing in inns or elsewhere. Such middlemen operated at margins, and helped by their gains from trade and their competition to integrate the domestic market, even in such bulky goods as cereals. Their needs, and their consequences, helped the development of the news-sheets and communications which by 1700 had made both producer and consumer more aware of regional differentials in price and/or product, and helped more rational market strategies to evolve. Transport and communications underpinned this development, but it is clear that while one may discern a trend towards more integrated markets, it is far from certain when it could be said to have matured. Trade was conducted along much more competitive and advanced lines in 1700, compared with 1500, but it was still relatively primitive compared with the advanced domestic market of the later eighteenth century. Our period saw the dwindling of fundamentally medieval methods of internal trading, and the growth of more advanced mercantile structures: but it saw neither the disappearance of the one, nor the triumph of the other.

5   Fluctuations and Intervention

A S in international commerce the impact of fluctuations and of the intervention of governments was also experienced in the home trades in the sixteenth and seventeenth centuries. Apart from Ashton's work on the eighteenth century, little interest has been shown in the cyclical movements of the pre-industrial economy, although Hoskins, and Braudel and Spooner, have discussed the topic in terms of price movements [72; 74; 75]. While scholars have shown interest in the general philosophies of state intervention in the economy, within this area the home trades have not yet received their due share of attention. Thus the basic fluctuations in the home trades, their determinants, and their relationship with the activities of the state await a detailed study. As with so many areas of this subject, many of the most interesting questions have yet to be answered.

(i)

Intervention in internal trade had characterised medieval government activities, from the simple municipal regulation of the market place to the more complex control of exports, or the imports of foodstuffs. Underlying such activities were a complex group of motives, which ranged from concepts of 'just price' or policies of protection for the consumer, to the policies of plenty, designed to ensure an adequate domestic supply of goods. To these basic tenets were added the quasi-governmental intervention in the economy by guilds, companies or other trade and manufacturing groups, which provided the quality control that formed the other side of the concept of a 'just price'. Not every member of the community had conformed willingly with these pressures to supply consumers at reasonable prices, and from time to time the government had been forced to legislate in the attempt to achieve the desired end.

These activities of the state continued and grew in the sixteenth century under the added pressures of agrarian problems and the Price Revolution. The middleman, the hoarder, the exporter and the forestaller all became the subjects of Tudor legislation. Sumptuary legislation, such as the act of 1563 which sought to strengthen the navy by increasing fisheries (5 Elizabeth, c. 5) [1, II, *110*], added to the range. Elements of industrial control, such as the Weavers Act of 1555 (2 & 3 Philip and Mary, c. 11) [1, I, *185*], and of monopoly, in manufacture or trade, completed the pattern. Beyond the formal law of such statutes were the proclamations which, at least to 1640, were held by the crown to have the same legal force, and which offered more immediate means of response to economic changes [2]. Two case-studies serve to illustrate the legal framework within which internal trade took place.

Bowden's work on wool is an obvious example. In this trade domestic and international regulations were operative virtually throughout our period. These controls were largely indirect in the first half of the sixteenth century, and were aimed at the preservation of the Staplers' monopoly, and at the enclosing grazier: legislation on the latter may have affected the marginal costs of expanding the output of fine wool, and clearly intensified the desire of the Staplers to control domestic competition. The act of 1552 (5 & 6 Edward VI, c. 7) was the result of this pressure. It set strict limits to the trade: only the staplers and manufacturers were allowed to deal in wool, and enforcement was left to informers. The act symbolised the twin errors of mid-Tudor lawmakers: their inability to allow local variants, and their anachronistic conservatism. Individual regions sought exemption from the act, and Halifax famously won the right to have its essential 'wool-drivers' restored in 1555 (2 & 3 Philip and Mary, c. 13) [1, I, *187*]. By the last quarter of the century the damaging effects of the statute were mitigated, and turned to profit, by the licensing of exemptions, the subjects of monopoly patents in the early seventeenth century. Although the export of wool was banned in 1614, the company of the Staplers, with that of the Woolmen, survived as a branch of regulated internal trade beyond the end of our period. The basic regulated trade, albeit freed from the restriction of legislation in 1624, remained throughout the seventeenth century, and was reinforced by proclamation and by the legislation of the years after 1660 against the free export of Irish wools and in favour of the hard-pressed home producer [36; 43]. Over all, intervention in this case seems to have done little to serve the cause of user or producer. The two centuries under study were a period in which the domestic wool trade struggled for the freedom needed for the essential woolfactors to operate effectively. Government intervention in the trade seems to have impaired efficiency without adding significantly to welfare.

Similarly mixed but enduring policies were visible in the corn trade. While there were medieval ordinances regulating the trade, it was in the early sixteenth century that activity rose with prices. Like the wool trade, corn-dealing was the subject of implicit statement in the agrarian legislation but the crucial break in institutional controls came in the 1550s. Two acts, against forestallers and middlemen in 1552 (5 & 6 Edward VI, c. 14) and regulating corn exports with threshold prices (1 & 2 Philip and Mary, c. 5) [1, I, 150], represented the response which was operative for the next century. As corn prices behaved in a volatile manner, these basic statutes were the objects of proclamations, which ordered enforcement or offered dispensations, or which ordered corn to market [2]. Frequently, either under the stimulus of a proclamation or on their own initiative, local authorities intervened directly in the market, suspending malting to release barley for bread, or ordering maltsters and millers to sell stocks to the public, sometimes at concessionary prices [35]. London and many lesser towns invested in their own granaries in this period, purchasing stocks at favourable times to employ them as equalisation funds in the retail market in time of dearth [34; 94]. After the middle of the seventeenth century, while regulation and statutory restrictions continued, plenty replaced dearth as the problem of the corn trade. Hence in 1673, and on a permanent basis from 1689, the state established bounties for export, the impact of which was felt internally, though to what extent is uncertain [82]. Direct and indirect consumer protection characterised the regulation of the corn trade, and this took the form of the harrying of middlemen, intervention in the market, and the control of external trades and internal uses. As in the wool trade, the benefits of regulation were unclear, and Everitt concludes that 'it is doubtful if the policy of regulation did not do as much harm as good' [35, 586].

(ii)

In the history of state intervention in domestic trades, it is clear that the 1540s and 1550s were crucial decades. The speed of price movements, of social and religious change, coincided with a counter-attack on behalf of the commonwealth by men like Latimer, Hales and Somerset, who represented a curious mixture of reaction, self-interest and positive planning [83; 84]. The period helps in the analysis of the objectives and the effects of the regulation of internal trade, which in its statutory form was largely the product of those years.

Many motives have been attributed to Tudor regulation. The simple reaction of the socially conscious to rapid economic change helped the cause of intervention, but so too did the heightening of economic analysis, which focused attention on the key elements in the economic and social problems of the day. In addition, Gras suggested that concern for the corn supply of the metropolis was vital to the regulation of the food trade [34; 87] and, more broadly, public order and the orderly ranking of an organic concept of society, the commonwealth, seem to have underpinned much of government action. All these influences, and the baser appeals of sectoral interests like the Staplers, contributed to the framework of law within which traders had to operate. But while it is clear that the disturbed years of the mid-sixteenth century produced a great burst of legislation, it seems less easy to demonstrate longer-term motives behind such moves. Furthermore, as Bindoff suggested, legislation was a protracted business and an inexact art [85]. The analysis of the causes of intervention may thus be rather less fruitful than that of its operative principles and effects.

Although legislation was framed in this period with helpful prefatory statements of policy objectives, such as that of the act restoring the enclosure statutes in 1597–8 (39 Elizabeth, c. 2) [1, 1, 84], generally speaking the legislative context was one of short-term need, not long-term purpose. The clustering of regulative statutes in the difficult years of the mid-sixteenth century suggests this, and the decade of the 1590s, in which harvest fluctuations produced dramatic changes in agrarian legislation, provides an extreme case of what Supple has called the fine-tuning of government activity to fluctuations in the economy [15]. If legislation can be broadly associated with short-run influences, then the less restricted form of lawmaking, the proclamation, can be tied more directly to the basic economic fluctuation, the harvest cycle, up to 1625. From 1485 to 1625, but concentrated in the middle fifty years of the sixteenth century, government issued or drafted some 209 proclamations relevant to domestic trade, excluding the currency. Their distribution correlates with swings of prices, as indicated by Hoskins's 'general average' for the harvest years [74; 75]. Pragmatism rather than principle appears to have guided such intervention, and this may help to account for the imprecision commonly the feature of the results. It is thus easy to understand the doubts expressed by Bowden and Everitt about the value of such intervention.

Of more immediate significance to the trader than the legal framework in which he was regulated in theory, was the reality of that control. How were such prolific enactments enforced? Again, data are imperfect, but Beresford's work on informers, who policed the penal statutes to 1640, and with particular enthusiasm in the subsequent twenty years, provides the material for assessing the motives of enforcement [86]. Over 17,000 offences, exclusive of customs, import and export matters, were informed upon in the Court of Exchequer up to 1659, and these represented a fair cross-section of the economic statutes in operation. Beresford demonstrated a general association of 'fat' and 'lean' years and the incidence of such informations, and our very crude correlation with the average of corn prices suggests a positive relationship, but not one of statistical significance. Such evidence confirms the impression derived from local informations to Quarter Sessions, and, more closely, the orders of municipalities for the release of corn like that of the Dorchester authorities in June 1630 which took corn from malting.[19] Recent work suggests that such action, if not effective in an economic sense, was vital as a part of social order [88]. The work of Ponko [87] is sufficient warning to us not to adopt simplistic interpretations of actions in the food trades of the period. But the fact remains that the evidence at present suggests that plenty or scarcity, expressed largely through food prices, does rather more to explain the fluctuations in the enforcement or use of statutes in the sixteenth and seventeenth centuries than any grand concepts of the rise and fall of an interventionist state.

(iii)

It is clear that no study of the internal trades of England in the sixteenth and seventeenth centuries can omit consideration of the role played by government. The subject awaits a full modern revision of the excellent but aged works of Gras and Westerfield, but some general assessment must be made here. Many factors helped to produce legislation, but the desire to curb mercantile excesses and to limit extremes of dearth, involving some positive planning, can be seen in the mid-sixteenth century. In the years after 1660, government showed an understandable sensitivity to the sectoral appeals of wool-growers and cereal farmers. But the over-all impression remains that the occasion, if not the explicit cause, for state intervention in trade was the movement of basic cycles in the economy. The twin extremes of dearth and plenty may have been more powerful than broadly interventionist philosophies, such as characterised the 1540s, 1550s and 1650s, or the quasi-fiscal uses of the penal statutes, such as the 'sale of nuisances' (the phrase is Pym's) of the 1630s. The study of the regulation of the inland trades does much to establish prag-matism rather than principle as an explanation of fluctuating state intervention in the period.

It is more difficult to assess the over-all economic effects of such activities. Bowden and Everitt inclined to the opinion that the imprecise and often myopic intervention of the state in basic factor markets did little for the welfare of consumers, and may have hindered the development of effective middleman net-works which could have redressed regional and local shortages with lower costs. The true antidote to views of the efficacy of intervention in such areas was Adam Smith's analysis of the corn-bounty system which, he suggested, did nothing for the welfare of farmers and served only to line the pockets of mer-chants.[20] Both these views seem severe. If the activity of central government in regulating internal trade can at best be regarded as neutral in its effect on the economy, then the role of local authorities in mitigating the worst excesses of the harvest cycle and in controlling the potential abuses of monopolistic middle-men must not be dismissed. In securing public order, it was essential that action should be seen to be taken, even if it was relatively ineffective [88]. Given the information available to sixteenth- and seventeenth-century governments, and the qual-ity of economic analysis which they were able to harness to decision-making, the probability is that freer internal trade would have distributed goods more effectively. But this would have been done at some cost to some consumers, which, in the hard years of the mid-sixteenth century, incurred the unaccept-able risk of disorder or rebellion. The final balance on this issue has yet to be cast, since the definitive study of the interaction of the state with the economy in this period awaits an author. The evidence of internal trade suggests that the effort should be made.

6 *Internal Trade and the Economy, 1500–1700*

IT would be asking too much for this survey of internal trade in the sixteenth and seventeenth centuries to offer firm conclusions. Too many questions remain as yet unanswered, and some unasked. Statements of greater certainty, given the work on the period by Willan and others, are possible for the seventeenth century, but much of the sixteenth century remains a dark age. In this context, for the years up to 1600 at least, the proper response of the student to suggestions here which imply some certainty is scepticism.

Although Everitt's work on agricultural markets before 1640 is available, the material for the more general study of domestic trade in the period is the product of past generations. The two major books, by Gras and Westerfield, were published in 1915. Problems seem to lie rather in explaining the lack of modern scholarly interest than in assessing the recent literature. Sources are, of course, poor, fragmented and discrete, rather like those for the other essential but untackled topic of the period, imports. But it may be that *a priori* the significance of the home market in the period has been underrated. Contemporary literature was much preoccupied with the external trades and their balances, and historians seem to have followed this. The immediate impressions of the period conjured up by the word 'trade' are those of external commerce – woollen exports, Anglo-Dutch rivalry, the re-export trades – and the conclusion here is that these impressions are misleading and that they may distort our understanding of the period.

Several reasons have been advanced for this view. It seems probable that even in the wool and cloth trades of the sixteenth century the role of the export market has been overstated. The nature of the home market for such goods must concern us as much as the conventional 'internal' aspects of the subject, the agrarian problem and employment. Because statistical data are available, scholars may have overstated the significance of the external account. Similar problems arise in the seventeenth century, and it seems possible that the impact of the colonial re-export trades before 1690 has been overstated. The obvious pattern of growth based on home trades must therefore be given its due place in the over-all assessment of the period. The image of internal trade in these years is therefore dull by reason of the quality of the glass held up to it, not its intrinsic interest and importance.

The student of trade in this period has to read widely to appreciate the extent and functions of internal commerce. Research by professional and amateur economic historians will lead to greater understanding, and in the context of so many gaps in our knowledge such new contributions will be of particular value. For the present, the proper conclusion should be that of the major apostle of the home trades and their importance, Daniel Defoe, prefaced by the word 'internal': 'Trade, like Religion, is what every Body talks of, but few understand' [5, 1].

Notes and References

Unless otherwise indicated, London is the place of publication. The abbreviation *E.H.R.* represents *Economic History Review*.

1. British Museum, Hargrave MSS. 321, p. 267 (1618–19), quoted in B. E. Supple, *Commercial Crisis and Change in England, 1600–42* (Cambridge, 1959).
2. J. F. Wright, 'British Economic Growth, 1688–1959', *E.H.R.*, 2nd ser., xviii (1965) pp. 397–412.
3. John Houghton, *A Collection for Improvement of Husbandry and Trade*, no. 118 (2 November 1694).
4. Ibid. no. 112 (21 September 1694).
5. Warwick Borough Records, W/13/1/3.
6. The 'Burns Journal' MS. of Gregory King, printed in P. Laslett (ed.), *Pioneers of Demography: The Earliest Classics* (Farnborough, 1973) p. 200.
7. Ibid. p. 214.
8. Butter priced at 20–22s. per firkin; cheese at 25–30s. per hundred. Both figures from Houghton, *Collection . . .* , vols v–viii.
9. I am indebted to Dr John Broad for this information.
10. M. W. Flinn, *Men of Iron: The Crowleys in the Early Iron Industry* (Edinburgh, 1962) pp. 34–45.
11. *North Riding Record Society*, vii (Sessions Records, 5 October 1705) p. 195.
12. 'Burns Journal', op. cit., p. 206.
13. C. L. Kingsford (ed.), *A Survey of London by John Stow*, 2 vols (Oxford, 1908) ii, pp. 282–3.
14. Public Record Office (P.R.O.): E/126/17, fos 16–17d.
15. P.R.O.: E/126/5, fos 77–78d.
16. P.R.O.: C/5/136/11.
17. P.R.O.: C/107/118.
18. J. A. Chartres, 'The Place of Inns in the Commercial Life of London and Western England, 1660–1760' (unpublished D.Phil. thesis, University of Oxford, 1973) p. 178.
19. C. H. Mayo (ed.), *The Municipal Records of the Borough of Dorchester, Dorset* (Exeter, 1908) p. 655.
20. Adam Smith, *An Inquiry into the Nature and Causes of the Wealth of Nations* (1776) book iv, ch. 5.

Select Bibliography

This is not an exhaustive book-list and it is confined to the most important works on the subject. General texts on the economic history of the period have been excluded. Unless otherwise indicated, London is the place of publication. The abbreviation *E.H.R.* represents *Economic History Review*.

I ORIGINAL SOURCES

[1] R. H. Tawney and E. Power, *Tudor Economic Documents*, 3 vols (1924). An invaluable collection, particularly strong on regulated trade.
[2] P. L. Hughes and J. F. Larkin, *Tudor Royal Proclamations*, 3 vols (New Haven, 1964–9).
[3] J. Thirsk and J. P. Cooper (eds), *Seventeenth-century Economic Documents* (Oxford, 1972). Contains a very useful section of materials on inland trade as well as the basic works of Gregory King.
[4] D. Defoe, *A Tour Through England and Wales*, 2 vols (1724–7; 1927). Perhaps the best, if unreliable, introduction to England, c. 1720.
[5] D. Defoe, *A Plan of English Commerce* (1728).
[6] D. Defoe, *The Complete English Tradesman* (1745: reprinted in one volume, New York, 1970). The great work on home trade, its methods, practices and scale, at the end of our period.
[7] G. E. Fussell (ed.), *Robert Loder's Farm Accounts, 1610–1620*, Camden Society, 3rd ser., LIII (1936). Offers remarkable insight into a farmer's marketing practices.
[8] C. B. Robinson (ed.), *Rural Economy in Yorkshire in 1641, being the Farming and Account Books of Henry Best of Elmswell in the East Riding*, Surtees Society, Durham, XXIII (1867). Better in some ways than [7] but not a satisfactory edition.
[9] J. D. Marshall (ed.), *The Autobiography of William Stout of Lancaster, 1665–1752* (Manchester, 1967). A shopkeeper's observations on trade and business life.

II GENERAL WORKS

[10] J. D. Gould, *Economic Growth in History* (1972).
[11] P. Deane and W. A. Cole, *British Economic Growth, 1688–1959*, 2nd ed. (Cambridge, 1967). An important book

with an assessment of the economy in the late seventeenth century.

[12] D. E. C. Eversley, 'The Home Market and Economic Growth in England, 1750–80', in E. L. Jones and G. E. Mingay (eds), *Land, Labour and Population in the Industrial Revolution: Essays Presented to J. D. Chambers* (1967). Contains ideas very relevant to the period before 1700.

[13] R. Davis, *English Overseas Trade, 1500–1700* (1973). A volume in this series, which is the briefest introduction to the subject.

[14] L. Stone, 'Elizabethan Overseas Trade', *E.H.R.*, 2nd ser., II (1949).

[15] B. E. Supple, *Commercial Crisis and Change in England, 1600–1642* (Cambridge, 1959). Perhaps the single most important volume on trade fluctuations and the cloth trade in the period.

[16] D. C. Coleman, *Industry in Tudor and Stuart England* (1975). An introductory survey of the subject, with much relevance to trade.

[17] J. Thirsk (ed.), *The Agrarian History of England and Wales*, IV (Cambridge, 1967). Of first importance, containing chapters on farming regions, techniques, enclosing, and labourers.

[18] E. Kerridge, *The Agricultural Revolution* (1967).

[19] J. C. Drummond and A. Wilbraham, *The Englishman's Food*, 2nd ed. (1957). An old book, but still the best general survey of consumption.

[20] E. A. Pratt, *A History of Inland Transport and Communication* (1912). Despite its age, one of the most shrewd and economical textbooks.

[21] J. Parkes, *Travel in England in the Seventeenth Century* (Oxford, 1925). Rather anecdotal, but full of useful information on home trade.

[22] W. T. Jackman, *The Development of Transportation in Modern England*, 2nd ed. (1962).

[23] T. C. Barker and C. I. Savage, *An Economic History of Transport in Britain*, 3rd ed. (1974). This and [22] are two reliable and informative textbooks on transport.

[24] B. R. Mitchell and P. Deane, *Abstract of British Historical Statistics* (Cambridge, 1962). A source for many of the known statistical series of the period, though largely concerned with the years after 1700.

[25] R. E. Zupko, *A Dictionary of English Weights and Measures* (Madison and London, 1968). An essential guide to the complex terms in which inland trade was conducted, with a valuable survey of legislation on weights and measures.

Land Carriage

[26] B. C. Jones, 'Westmorland Pack-horse Men in Southampton', *Transactions of the Cumberland and Westmorland Antiquarian and Archaeological Society*, LIX (1960). An important account of long-distance carriage from the north-west in the years 1450–1550.

[27] J. A. Chartres, 'Road Carrying in England in the Seventeenth Century: Myth and Reality', *E.H.R.*, 2nd ser., XXX (1977). Reconsiders the functions and extent of public carriers in the years from 1637.

[28] W. Albert, *The Turnpike Road System in England, 1663–1840* (Cambridge, 1972). An important modern revision of the subject.

[29] M. J. T. Lewis, *Early Wooden Railways* (1970). A detailed account of wagonways from the sixteenth century onwards.

Water Transport

[30] R. Davis, *The Rise of the English Shipping Industry in the Seventeenth and Eighteenth Centuries*, 2nd impression (Newton Abbot, 1972). Rather thin before 1700, and on coastwise shipping, but the only comprehensive account.

[31] T. S. Willan, *The English Coasting Trade, 1600–1750* (Manchester, reprint with new preface, 1967). Nearly forty years old, but still the only book on the subject, it is essential reading.

[32] T. S. Willan, *River Navigation in England, 1600–1760* (Oxford, 1936). The other half of his study of water transport, and almost equally alone in the field.

[33] J. R. Ward, *The Finance of Canal Building in Eighteenth-Century England* (Oxford, 1974). Contains an evaluation of river navigation, and critique of [32].

IV TRADES IN AGRICULTURAL COMMODITIES

[34] N. S. B. Gras, *The Evolution of the English Corn Market, from the Twelfth to the Eighteenth Century*, Harvard Economic Studies, XIII (Cambridge, 1915). One of the major works on the subject, little challenged in its overall scope by subsequent research.

[35] A. M. Everitt, 'The Marketing of Agricultural Produce', in [17]. The major survey of the subject from 1500 to 1640, and basic reading for modern interpretations.

[36] P. J. Bowden, *The Wool Trade in Tudor and Stuart England*

(1962). One of the few modern monographs on specific trades, and strong on the role of government intervention.

[37] G. E. Fussell, *The English Dairy Farmer, 1500–1900* (1966).

[38] W. M. Stern, 'Cheese Shipped Coastwise to London towards the Middle of the Eighteenth Century', *Guildhall Miscellany,* IV (1973). One of two important articles on the trade which helps to understand the position in the late seventeenth century.

[39] M. L. Ryder, 'The History of Sheep Breeds in Britain', *Agricultural History Review,* XII (1964). Adds to the account in [36].

[40] A. R. B. Haldane, *The Drove Roads of Scotland* (1952). The best of the older books on droving, with discussion of some aspects of Welsh, as well as Scots, traffics.

[41] C. A. J. Skeel, 'The Cattle Trade between Wales and England from the Fifteenth to the Nineteenth Centuries', *Transactions of the Royal Historical Society,* 4th ser., IX (1926).

[42] P. G. Hughes, *Wales and the Drovers* (1943). Two rather old and unsatisfactory accounts of Welsh drovers.

[43] D. M. Woodward, 'The Anglo-Irish Livestock Trade of the Seventeenth Century', *Irish Historical Studies,* XVIII (1973). An important article on this substantial but short-lived trade.

[44] P. V. McGrath, 'The Marketing of Food, Fodder, and Livestock in the London Area in the Seventeenth Century', unpublished M.A. thesis, London University, 1948. An indispensable work, but of limited circulation. Adds to [91–3].

[45] A. H. John, 'The Course of Agricultural Change, 1660–1760' in L. S. Pressnell (ed.), *Studies in the Industrial Revolution: Essays Presented to T. S. Ashton* (1960). Surveys the trends in agriculture and food trade from the mid-seventeenth century.

V THE TEXTILE TRADES

[46] N. Lowe, *The Lancashire Textile Industry in the Sixteenth Century,* Chetham Society, 3rd ser., XX (1972).

[47] A. P. Wadsworth and J. de L. Mann, *The Cotton Trade and Industrial Lancashire, 1600–1780* (Manchester, 1931). This and [46] are two accounts of the same region containing detailed assessments of factors and internal trades.

[48] D. W. Jones, 'The "Hallage" Receipts of the London Cloth Markets, 1562–*c.*1720', *E.H.R.,* 2nd ser., XXV (1972). An attempt to analyse cloth sales through the statistics of the

Blackwell Hall market, which aids assessment of the home trades.

VI MINERAL AND METAL TRADES

[49] J. U. Nef, *The Rise of the British Coal Industry*, 2 vols (1932). A massive work which has as its theme the revolution in the coal trade. Invaluable when treated sceptically.

[50] J. Langton, 'Coal Output in South-west Lancashire, 1590–1799', *E.H.R.*, 2nd ser., xxv (1972). A coalfield study which helps to put [49] in perspective.

[51] G. Hammersley, 'The Charcoal Iron Industry and its Fuel, 1540–1750', *E.H.R.*, 2nd ser., xxvi (1973).

[52] B. L. C. Johnson, 'The Charcoal Iron Industry in the Early Eighteenth Century', *Geographical Journal*, cxvii (1951).

[53] B. L. C. Johnson, 'The Foley Partnerships: the Iron Industry at the End of the Charcoal Era', *E.H.R.*, 2nd ser., iv (1952).

[54] M. W. Flinn, 'The Growth of the English Iron Industry, 1660–1760', *E.H.R.*, 2nd ser., xi (1958). The four articles [51–54] present the divided structure of the iron industry and its trade consequences.

[55] W. H. B. Court, *The Rise of the Midland Industries, 1600–1838* (1938). A fine regional study which analyses trade connections in some detail.

[56] M. B. Rowlands, *Masters and Men in the West Midland Metalware Trades before the Industrial Revolution* (Manchester, 1975). Adds individual merchants and producers to the analysis of [55].

[57] G. R. Lewis, *The Stannaries* (Boston, 1908).

[58] J. Hatcher, *English Tin Production and Trade Before 1550* (Oxford, 1973). Strong on the early domestic trades.

[59] H. Hamilton, *The English Brass and Copper Industries to 1800* (1926).

[60] E. Hughes, *Studies in Administration and Finance, 1558–1815* (Manchester, 1934). Chs 2, 3, and 9 represent the only basic work on the salt trade.

VII OTHER INDUSTRIAL TRADES

[61] L. A. Clarkson, 'The Organization of the English Leather Industry in the Late Sixteenth and Seventeenth Centuries', *E.H.R.*, 2nd ser., xiii (1960). Strong on the trades consequential on the division of labour in the industry.

[62] L. A. Clarkson, 'The Leather Crafts in Tudor and Stuart England', *Agricultural History Review*, xiv (1966). Better than [61] on leather-supply networks.

[63] D. W. Crossley, 'The Performance of the Glass Industry in Sixteenth-Century England', *E.H.R.*, 2nd ser., xxv (1972).
[64] E. S. Godfrey, *The Development of English Glassmaking, 1560–1640* (Oxford, 1975). This and [63] assess the industrial consequences of distribution problems.

VIII MARKETING AGENCIES AND INSTITUTIONS

[65] R. B. Westerfield, 'Middlemen in English Business: Particularly Between 1660 and 1760', *Transactions of the Connecticut Academy of Arts and Sciences*, xix (1915; reprinted Newton Abbot, 1968). Like [34] still the only book in the field, and while somewhat modified by [35] a remarkable analysis of factors in the period.
[66] T. S. Willan, *The Inland Trade* (Manchester, 1976). A valuable collection of papers relating to internal trade.
[67] D. Davis, *A History of Shopping* (1966). An overview of the subject, based largely on secondary materials.
[68] D. Alexander, *Retailing in England During the Industrial Revolution* (1970). Includes a survey of the historical background to his subject.
[69] A. M. Everitt, 'The English Urban Inn, 1560–1760', in Everitt (ed.), *Perspectives in English Urban History* (1973). A useful synopsis of the many functions of the inn in the period.
[70] J. A. Chartres, 'Markets and Marketing in Metropolitan Western England in the Late Seventeenth and Eighteenth Centuries', in M. A. Havinden (ed.), *Husbandry and Marketing in the South-west, 1500–1800* (University of Exeter, 1973). A regional study of changing market organisation.

IX CREDIT, FINANCE, AND PRICES

[71] R. B. Outhwaite, *Inflation in Tudor and Early Stuart England* (1969). A short survey of the problem.
[72] F. P. Braudel and F. Spooner, 'Prices in Europe from 1450 to 1750', in E. E. Rich and C. H. Wilson (eds), *Cambridge Economic History of Europe*, iv (Cambridge, 1967).
[73] C. W. J. Granger and C. M. Elliott, 'A Fresh Look at Wheat Prices and Markets in the Eighteenth Century', *E.H.R.*, 2nd ser., xx (1967). An important article, related to the matter of [45] and [70].
[74] W. G. Hoskins, 'Harvest Fluctuations and English Economic History, 1480–1619', *Agricultural History Review*, xii (1964).
[75] W. G. Hoskins, 'Harvest Fluctuations and English Economic History, 1620–1759', *Agricultural History Review*, xvi (1968).

This and [74] are important works, based on Exeter data, on harvest cycles.

[76] C. J. Harrison, 'Grain Price Analysis and Harvest Qualities, 1465–1635', *Agricultural History Review*, XIX (1971). A critique of the methods and conclusions of [74] and [75].

[77] T. S. Ashton, *Economic Fluctuations in England, 1700–1800* (1959). The most extended account of fluctuations in the pre-industrial economy, with many concepts relevant to this period.

[78] M. M. Postan, 'Credit in Medieval Trade', *E.H.R.*, I (1928) reprinted in E. M. Carus-Wilson, *Essays in Economic History*, I (1954). A seminal article, whose relevance extends throughout our period.

[79] H. J. Habakkuk, 'The Long-term Rate of Interest and the Price of Land in the Eighteenth Century', *E.H.R.*, 2nd ser., V (1952). Surveys longer-term aspects of credit, but no longer wholly acceptable.

[79a] B. A. Holderness, 'Credit in English Rural Society before the Nineteenth Century, with special reference to the period 1650–1720', *Agricultural History Review*, XXIV (1976). An important survey, the early conclusions of a major research project.

X GOVERNMENT, REGULATION, AND PUBLIC ORDER

[80] F. Clifford, *A History of Private Bill Legislation*, 2 vols (1888–9). A remarkable book, principally relevant to transport improvement.

[81] L. A. Harper, *The English Navigation Laws: A Seventeenth-Century Experiment in Social Engineering* (1939; reprinted New York, 1973). Valuable for its estimates of shipping, to be read with [30].

[82] D. G. Barnes, *A History of the English Corn Laws, 1660–1846* (1930). Retrospective chapter covers our period, and later work examines the Corn Bounties and their effect.

[83] W. R. D. Jones, *The Tudor Commonwealth, 1529–59* (1970). A valuable study of the attitudes current in the mid-sixteenth century.

[84] R. H. Tawney, *Religion and the Rise of Capitalism* (1926). Much-criticised, but the best account of the targets of the 'Commonwealth men'.

[85] S. T. Bindoff, 'The Making of the Statute of Artificers', in Bindoff *et al.* (ed.), *Elizabethan Government and Society* (1961). An important assessment of the mechanics of Tudor legislation.

[86] M. W. Beresford, 'The Common Informer, the Penal Statutes, and Economic Regulation', *E.H.R.*, 2nd ser., x (1957). A study of the principal method of the enforcement of legislation in economic affairs.

[87] V. Ponko Jr, 'N. S. B. Gras and Elizabethan Corn Policy: A Re-examination', *E.H.R.*, 2nd ser., xvii (1964). An important critique of the metropolitan bias of [34].

[88] J. Walter and K. Wrightson, 'Dearth and the Social Order in Early Modern England', *Past and Present*, 71 (1976). Joins with [35] in rehabilitating government activity as a means to curbing disorder.

XI REGIONAL AND LOCAL STUDIES

[89] T. C. Smout, *Scottish Trade on the Eve of Union, 1660–1707* (Edinburgh, 1963). A valuable survey of seventeenth-century Scottish trade connections.

[90] C. W. Chalklin, *Seventeenth-century Kent* (1965). An excellent study of an important maritime county, with a detailed assessment of internal trading.

[91] F. J. Fisher, 'The Development of the London Food Market, 1540–1640', *E.H.R.*, v (1935), reprinted in E. M. Carus-Wilson, *Essays in Economic History*, i (1954).

[92] F. J. Fisher, 'The Development of London as a Centre of Conspicuous Consumption in the Sixteenth and Seventeenth Centuries', *Transactions of the Royal Historical Society*, 4th ser., xxx (1948), reprinted in E. M. Carus-Wilson, *Essays* ii (1962).

[93] E. A. Wrigley, 'A Simple Model of London's Importance in Changing English Society and Economy, 1650–1750', *Past and Present*, 37 (1967). This, [91] and [92] are three important articles on the impact of the capital on trade and on the economy in general.

[94] D. M. Palliser, 'York under the Tudors: the Trading Life of the Northern Capital', in A. M. Everitt (ed.), *Perspectives in English Urban History* (1973). Much concerned with inland trade and mercantile relationships.

[95] D. M. Woodward, *The Trade of Elizabethan Chester* (Hull, 1970). Contains much information on internal trades, inland trade links, and commodities traded between Chester and Ireland.

[96] D. G. Hey, *An English Rural Community: Myddle under the Tudors and Stuarts* (Leicester, 1974).

[97] M. Spufford, *Contrasting Communities: English Villagers in the*

Sixteenth and Seventeenth Centuries (Cambridge, 1974). This and [96] are important recent studies of village communities, which include many important details of internal trade and credit structures.

Index

78